COUNTRY
DOUGHCRAFTS

COUNTRY DOUGHCRAFTS

50 ORIGINAL PROJECTS TO BUILD YOUR MODELING SKILLS

SOPHIE-JANE TILLEY AND SUSAN WELBY

MEREDITH® PRESS

For Adrienne, Alex and Jake

First published in Great Britain in 1995 by Hamlyn
an imprint of Reed Consumer Books Limited,
Michelin House, 81 Fulham Road, London SW3 6RB

U.S. edition published by
Meredith® Press
150 E. 52nd Street, New York, NY 10022

Meredith® Press is an imprint of Meredith® Books:
President, Book Group: Joseph J. Ward
Vice President, Editorial Director: Elizabeth P. Rice

EDITOR: **NINA SHARMAN**
ART EDITOR: **PRUE BUCKNALL**
PRODUCTION: **MICHELLE THOMAS**
EXECUTIVE EDITOR: **JUDITH MORE**
EXECUTIVE ART EDITOR: **LARRAINE SHAMWANA**
ART DIRECTOR: **JACQUI SMALL**
PHOTOGRAPHY: **MICHELLE GARRETT**, STEP-BY-STEP PHOTOGRAPHY: **POLLY WREFORD**
CRAFTS: **SOPHIE JANE TILLEY**, TEXT: **SUSAN WELBY**

For Meredith® Press:
Executive Editor: **Maryanne Bannon**
Senior Editor: **Carol Spier**
Assistant Editor: **Bonita M. Eckhaus**
Technical Editor: **Ellen W. Liberles**

All correspondence should be addressed to Meredith® Press.

ISBN (hardcover) 0-696-20460-6
(softcover) 0-696-20461-4
LOC 95-077460

Produced by Mandarin Offset
Printed and bound in China

Distributed by Meredith Corporation, Des Moines, Iowa

CONTENTS

NATURE'S GIFTS 22

ESSENTIAL ELEMENTS 40

STYLE FILE 52

CONTENTS

INTRODUCTION

The urge to model, bake, and decorate dough is as traditional and as widespread as the practice of making bread itself. The ancient Egyptians, Romans, and Greeks made dough figure offerings to their gods, and modeling dough decorations to commemorate religious festivals (particularly Christmas) is still a popular pastime in many countries. Brightly colored dough designs are sold in market stalls in South America, and tourist centers in Shanghai still demonstrate the traditional art of making enchanting dolls from twists of dyed dough. Salt dough modeling is enjoying a revival in the U.S.A, and dough objects are beginning to make an appearance in British gift shops once again.

The availability of more sophisticated modeling materials, like ready-made and non bake clays may have contributed to the decline in popularity of salt dough. Convenience is bound to appeal to busy crafters, but the price of some modeling materials can be restricting. Salt dough ingredients are very inexpensive to buy and quick to prepare, which means that you can afford to be adventurous in size and quantity and relaxed about the occasional mistake.

The projects in this book are meant to provide you with ideas, not hard-and-fast rules—so feel free to vary the designs and to add your own finishing touches. Suggestions about special paint effects, textures, cutouts and alternative finishes are included in the introductions to many of the projects—use the photographs and instructions as guide-lines, and your own ideas should soon develop along with your skill.

The standard items used for each craft can be found in most kitchens and any extra equipment mentioned is widely available. To give you more choice (and scope for invention), alternative or additional materials and tools are suggested wherever possible.

Hand-modeling is unpredictable by nature, so do think twice before throwing any "mistakes" away. If you are prepared to highlight, rather than hide, slight variations and quirks, your work will be more original and unique to you. Aiming for perfection can be inhibiting, so relax and try not to see every flaw as a failure—production-line perfection isn't terribly inspiring and often lacks the charm and beauty of a handmade craft.

Materials and Techniques

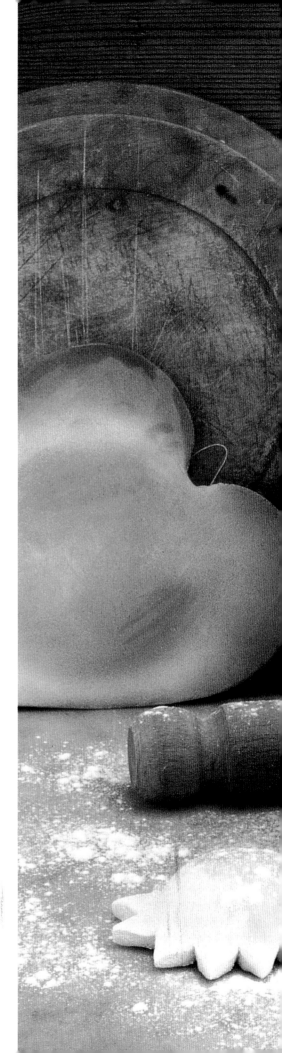

This section will give you a thorough grounding in all aspects of doughcraft—from preparing the dough to applying high-lights and decorative paint effects. Refer to this section whenever you have doubts or questions about modeling, relief work and baking—or simply browse through it to refresh your memory before embarking on the next project. Obviously, you want your doughcrafts to look as good as possible, but don't be discouraged by unexpected results. Small flaws can add interesting dimensions to a project and an "accident" may produce an original texture or an unusual surface finish.

MAKING THE DOUGH

This book uses a traditional salt dough mixture for all its projects. It is easier to stick to one recipe and, when made up and handled properly, this simple salt, flour, and water mixture is very successful and extremely adaptable; it also behaves with a certain predictability, which is reassuring, especially when you are embarking on new projects.

Salt is an effective hardening agent. Although some experts add cooking oil or even wallpaper paste to their dough mixtures for extra smoothness and strength, the recipe below produces an excellent dough which handles and hardens successfully, without the addition of extra ingredients.

The basic recipe makes enough dough for one small project and two larger ones (a few small decorations with relief work and two bowls, for example). This may seem a lot, but baking more than one object at a time makes good economical and ecological sense. For less, or more dough, simply halve or double the ingredients given in the basic recipe accordingly. As a general rule, you should always use half the amount of salt to flour.

Ingredients

FLOUR—Standard all-purpose flour is used throughout this book. Use good-quality flour; cheaper brands may be difficult to handle and can also vary widely in degrees of absorbency. You will quickly become accustomed to the look and feel of the dough you make, so once you have decided on a brand of flour, stay with it. Whole wheat flour produces interesting textured effects,

but it tends to be heavier to handle and takes longer to bake than the all-purpose variety. Self-rising flour puffs up in the oven and should never be used for doughcraft.

SALT—As long as it is finely granulated, the cheapest table salt available makes good dough.

You will need
- Large mixing bowl
- Measuring cup
- Water
- Cool surface for kneading

THE BASIC RECIPE
- Two level cups of all-purpose flour
- One level cup of table salt
- About ½ cup of lukewarm water

Method

Pour the flour and salt into a mixing bowl and combine thoroughly. Gradually add enough water to knead the mixture into a pliable ball. This may take more, or less, than the ½ cup of water in the recipe (depending on the flour and the temperature of the room). Judge the exact amount of water by feel—if the mixture is too sticky, add a little more flour. If it crumbles, add more water.

Kneading

The more you knead it, the smoother and more pliable salt dough becomes. Work the dough for at least ten minutes with slow, rhythmic movements, pushing it away from you with the heels of your hands, then folding it back on itself. Repeat the process again and again, turning the whole wad of dough regularly. Well-prepared dough is firm, malleable, and elastic enough to

stretch into a soft, slightly bouncy "rope" when gently pulled.

Rolling out dough

For flat pieces, roll out the dough to a uniform thickness, using a strip of wood (of the proper thickness) along each side of the dough. (For instance, use ¼-in. lattice strips to roll ¼-in. thick dough.) Flatten the dough until the rolling pin rolls evenly along the wooden strips.

For round decorations, roll a piece of dough between your palms to form a ball, using enough dough to make the ball into the size specified. For rounded, but more elongated shapes, use your fingers to roll the dough on a flat surface to form a sausage-shaped roll the size specified. Use your fingers to press and shape the pieces as the directions indicate.

Storing raw dough

Take as much dough as you need for the project, wrap the rest in plastic wrap (or seal in an airtight container), and store it in the refrigerator. When you are ready to use it, bring the stored dough back to room temperature by kneading it thoroughly.

TIPS

- Make sure that your working environment is not too warm. (The dough becomes soft, sticky, and moist in an overheated room).
- Keep your hands as cool and dry as possible when working with dough.
- Always work on a cool, dry surface.
- Dough gets soggy quite quickly and doesn't store well for more than a day (or two days at the most), so make only as much as you can reasonably use.
- While modeling a project place a dry cloth over any dough you are not actually working with; use a damp cloth when the dough needs moistening.

DOUGH PASTE

Dough paste plays an important part in doughcraft. It only takes seconds to prepare, so mix a fresh batch for each new project. A small, $\frac{1}{8}$ in. paintbrush is suitable for most pasting jobs. Although a nylon-bristled brush is perfectly adequate, the bristles should not be too stiff (in case they indent the dough) or too loose (in case the strands fall out). Apply the paste to raw dough in small amounts. If you paint on too much, your dough will become soggy and unmanageable.

The thickness of the paste depends on the consistency needed for various techniques, but a watery mixture (to attach and seal dough pieces) is standard for all projects. Mix a thin paste and keep it on hand as you work—mix a thicker paste if and when you need it.

To attach relief work and decorations to a project, apply the paste sparingly to the underside of the shape to be attached. Then paint a little dough paste on the base area and join the two pieces together. To fill gaps between the base and relief work, brush thicker dough paste into gaps until no joints are visible. If necessary, smooth over with a little plain water, applied with a paintbrush. You can also use dough paste to correct mistakes. For example, if you need to cover indentations or surface scoring, brush a thicker paste over the affected area and smooth over the surface with a small spatula or a damp pastry brush. See also FILLING AND REPAIRING on page 18.

To make dough paste

- When you have prepared your raw dough, tear off a peanut-sized piece of dough (for larger amounts of paste, tear off a bigger lump of dough).
- To make a standard, watery paste, put the dough into a saucer or lid and add lukewarm water, drop by drop. Mix until the dough becomes tacky and then add more water to thin it out.
- For a thicker paste, use the same method, but stop adding water when the paste is a soft, buttery consistency.

MATERIALS AND EQUIPMENT

The materials and equipment needed for individual projects are given, but you may find a general list useful too. Most materials and equipment can be found around the house or at local hardware stores.

Standard list
- Salt dough
- Dough paste
- Cardboard for templates
- Nonstick baking sheet(s) (the raised edges on a baking tray can get in the way)
- Ruler (for measuring dough thickness; a ruler also makes a good cutter)
- Rolling pin
- Small kitchen knife
- Small wooden spatula, or flat, paddle-shaped modeling tool (for patting and smoothing surfaces)
- Small paintbrush (for dough paste)

You will also need *(For certain projects)*
- A long-bladed knife or pizza cutting wheel (for cutting long strips of dough)
- Lids of various sizes (round cookie cutters or small glasses can also be used)
- Ovenproof bowls to use as molds
- Cookie or canape cutters (to use as alternatives to templates)
- Pastry brush (to smooth surfaces)
- Tweezers (for handling small beads)
- Cotton swabs
- Wire, 18-gauge (for hanging loops and threading), 24-gauge (for decoration)
- Wire cutters
- Round-ended pliers
- Small mirror (mirror glass can be cut to size, or use old mirrors)
- Cork tiles or felt for backing
- Craft glue
- Aluminum foil
- Loose beads, decorative buttons
- Dried cloves (for decoration)

MODELING DECORATIONS

Surface decoration adds interest and texture to your work. Wherever possible, try to work on the baking sheet itself; this keeps the backs of your salt dough pieces smooth (and transferring soft dough pieces from one surface to another can distort their shapes).

Do not add flour, water, or grease to the baking sheet. If your dough has been prepared well, it should slide off the baking sheet easily when baked. If you must move any raw dough pieces, do so carefully, using a wide spatula.

MODELING SHELLS

These shells decorate the Shell Box on pages 50–1. Once you've picked up the general technique, you could try improvising with a wider range of sea creatures. For example, starfish can be made with cookie cutters (or you could model them by hand).

To make cockleshells (scallops)
1 Flatten a ball of dough into a fat disk.

2 Pinching one end between the thumb and forefinger of one hand, gently press the opposite end into a fan shape.

3 Use a small knife to make shallow cuts on the surface of the shell and then score around the edges.

To make cochlea (snail or screwshells)
1 Roll a ball of dough into a short sausage.

2 Gently turn one end two or three times until it forms a spiral.

3 Use your finger to indent the other end and lift it upward to make an opening. Smaller shells can be made from small balls of dough, indented in the middle and pinched at both ends.

MODELING AND ARRANGING LEAVES

Leaves and petals are used to decorate many of the doughcraft projects in this book. The trick is to make them look as natural as possible. If you are modeling by hand, don't try to produce exactly the same leaf or petal every time, but vary their shapes and sizes.

If you are using templates to cut out leaves, their shapes will obviously be the same, but you can arrange them to look as realistic as possible.

Arranging and attaching leaves

Salt dough leaves look best when they are arranged in a natural way (see Grapevine Basket, pages 26–9). Avoid laying leaves in flat, regimented lines – instead, add life to your arrangements by overlapping parts of some leaves and squeezing and twisting the tips of others. Leaves also look very attractive when draped over the edges of plaques and bowls. A small amount of dough paste is usually enough to attach raw dough decorations to a base shape, but you may find it useful to brush a little thickened dough paste on the underside of larger leaves (to reinforce any weak areas). Use thickened dough paste to fill gaps between shapes and to brush over any cracks.

To make vine leaves with a template

Roll the dough out to a thickness of about ¼ in. Lay the vine leaf template (see page 130) on top of the dough and cut around it carefully. Smooth any rough edges. Add veins by gently pressing the knife blade into the dough. Score the vertical center line first, then add veins on each side of this line, working outward. When each scored line reaches the edge of the dough, press in to indent. With your thumb and forefinger, twist the ends of the leaves and tease them upward to vary their shapes.

To hand-model leaves

1 Flatten a small piece of dough. Either shape the leaf by hand, or cut and trim it into shape with a small knife. Smooth edges with the flat side of a knife blade or with a small spatula.

2 Add veins by gently pressing the blade of a small knife into the dough. Score the vertical center line first, then add veins on each side of this line. Where the scored lines reach the edge of the dough, press in to indent (this produces a fluted effect along the edges of the leaf).

OTHER DECORATIVE TECHNIQUES

Scoring the surface of salt dough is a technique used throughout this book. Not only is it a good way of adding texture and interest to salt dough, but it also provides attractive contrast lines when you come to paint the finished project. Press the blade of a small kitchen knife gently across the surface of the dough.

Indenting the dough (with the end of a small paintbrush or with a toothpick) produces shallow holes which can be painted or used as sockets for decorative beads and small balls of salt dough. The point of a knife will produce smaller, sharper indentations. Indenting is also a useful way of creating features when modeling faces (see Gift for a New Baby, pages 126–7).

Flattening and patting edges and surfaces with a small, damp wooden spatula gives a smoother finish.

Cutouts are simply shapes made with cookie cutters, lids from small jars, or the rims of small glasses. Over-moist dough produces torn edges and soggy results, so make sure that the dough is flexible but not floppy before cutting your shape.

MAKING WIRE LOOPS

A piece of wire, embedded in a salt dough base, makes an effective hanging loop for displaying salt dough wreaths, frames, and decorations. Wire loops can also be used to join or reinforce separate dough pieces. Loops of thinner, more flexible wire can be embedded in the backs of frames to anchor photographs in place (see Patchwork Frame, pages 56–7).

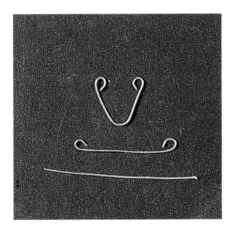

To make hanging loops

Cut a piece of 18-gauge wire about 2³⁄₄ in. long. Using round-ended pliers, curve the wire and curl each end into an open O shape.

Push the loop into the dough base until both curled ends are hidden.

MOLDING

Draping dough over a raised surface adds a new dimension to modeling work. It brings otherwise flat shapes to life and responds beautifully to surface decoration. The secret of successful molding lies in the preparation. Knead your dough thoroughly to give it a pliable, almost elastic quality.

Molded projects involve "half-baking". Simply bake the outside of the project until it has taken on the shape of the mold. When it is firm enough to handle (but still only half-baked), remove the mold and return the project to the oven to bake the inside. This process is described in more detail on the opposite page.

Molding over foil shapes

Raw salt dough is extremely flexible, which means that it is perfectly suited to molding over aluminum foil. This book uses various foil molds to make containers and other decorative items. Molds are made by scrunching sheets of foil into compact wads of various shapes (see the Molded Moon above and on pages 46–7). The instructions for the relevant projects will give you an idea of the height and width of the shapes used, but as a general rule, use enough foil to squeeze into a densely-packed shape (strong enough to support the dough during baking). If your mold is too large, squeeze harder to reduce its size, or tear off the excess foil. If it is too small, add more foil.

Molding over ovenproof containers

Ovenproof bowls and dishes of various shapes and sizes make excellent salt dough molds. The instructions for the relevant projects will supply you with approximate dimensions, but as long as the bowl or dish you choose is the right shape, you can vary the size of the project by using a larger or smaller container. Ovenproof bowls with textured patterns, lipped edges, or handles should be avoided.

The molding technique itself is very straightforward. Just cover the outside of an ovenproof bowl with foil. Tuck the foil inside the bowl — the overlap should be about 2 in.— and smooth the foil over the outside of the bowl until it is as flat and as wrinkle-free as possible. Roll your dough out to the correct thickness, carefully drape it over the ovenproof container, and trim around the edges (see the Ethnic Bowl above and on pages 64–7).

BAKING

Salt dough baking is not an exact science. Ovens differ and cooking times may vary according to the thickness of a project, the number of projects baked at one time, and the type of fuel used. When you have baked a few projects, you will have a better idea of exact baking times, according to the way your own oven performs.

Raw salt dough is rolled out to two standard thicknesses throughout this book. These are either ¼ in. or ⅜ in. The information on the right will give you an idea of the oven settings needed to bake projects with these standard base thicknesses. Bear in mind that relief work makes an object thicker, lengthening the baking process; because of this, approximate baking times for certain types of projects (heavily decorated, molded, and/or woven) are also listed.

If you are in any doubt, err on the side of caution. Baking slowly on a low oven setting protects against distortion. A slow, steady baking process will give you an idea of the way dough looks and feels as it hardens.

Preheat the oven and place your baking sheet of uncooked dough onto the middle shelf. Use the oven temperatures and times printed right as a general guide, but don't worry too much about being exact. Your own judgment should soon tell you whether an object is done, especially if you use the tap test.

The tap test
As the dough cooks, it begins to harden and the surface starts to look drier and lighter in color. When you think it's done, tap the object with your finger. If it sounds hollow, carefully slide a long-bladed knife or spatula underneath to loosen it. Using an oven glove, turn the dough over carefully and tap its base. A hard texture and a hollow sound tell you that the object is ready (a spongy texture and a dull, thudding noise means that it needs more time in the oven).

APPROXIMATE BAKING TIMES AND TEMPERATURES

Thinner objects—¼ in. thick
300° (slow) for 3–4 hours

Thicker objects—⅜ in. thick
300° (slow) for 6–7 hours

NOTE:
Convection ovens tend to bake salt dough more quickly during the early stages. Take care to check your dough regularly.

Projects decorated with solid pieces of dough relief, such as the Traditional Fruit Basket (pages 36–7) and the Christmas Wreath (pages 91–3), will take about 10–12 hours to bake. Solid, hand-modeled items, such as the African Dolls (pages 70–5) and the Cherub Christmas decoration (page 89) should be baked for about 6–7 hours.

Cooling
Simply remove your baked project (on its baking sheet) from the oven and set aside to cool down. Avoid handling until cool (unless repair work is necessary—see page 18). In the case of projects with mirrors (for example, the

Mermaid Mirror, pages 48–9) the oven should be turned off after baking and the project allowed to cool down gradually inside the oven. Avoid extreme changes in atmosphere. If you have to move the dough to another room, for example, make sure that it is not exposed to steam, damp, or cold. The dough must be allowed to cool completely before you paint or varnish it.

HALF-BAKING
All projects that use molds need to be half-baked on the mold, then completely baked off it: Bake the project on the mold until the surface is dry-looking, and firm enough to handle without distorting its shape or damaging its structure. Take it from the oven (close the oven door to retain heat), remove the mold, and return the piece to the oven to finish baking through. Take care when handling half-baked dough.

For projects baked on molds without relief work, such as the Ethnic Bowl (pages 64–7) and the Molded Hearts (pages 106–11), bake for about 4 hours at 300° (slow) before taking from the oven and removing the mold. Return to the oven for another 2½–3 hours to finish baking.

For projects with thick relief work, such as the Shell Box (pages 50–1), add an extra ¹⁄₂ hour to the baking time before removing the foil mold, and about another hour to the final stage of baking.

For larger projects with thick relief work, such as the Hen Lid (pages 80–1), add at least 1 hour to the baking time before removing the mold, and approximately 1 more hour to the final stage of baking.

Where half-baked components are attached to raw dough bases, for example, the Shell Box (pages 50–1) and the Horn of Plenty (pages 96–9), bake for about 4¹⁄₂ hours before removing the mold. After attaching the top to the base, return to the oven for about another 6 hours to finish baking.

Open-weave, molded projects, such as the Grapevine Basket (pages 26–9) and the Hen Nest (page 82), should be baked for about 6 hours, then the molds removed and the projects returned to the oven for about 4–5 hours to finish baking.

BROWNING

This technique produces different degrees of color, from pale gold to deep brown. Bake your project completely. Leaving the oven on, remove the cooked dough and make a mental note of its surface color. Decide how much deeper you would like the color to be. (Browning can happen quickly, so making decisions now will help you to react quickly and decisively when the dough reaches the right shade.)

Turn the oven up to the next setting. Return the project to the oven and watch closely as the increased heat deepens its color. (If your oven has no

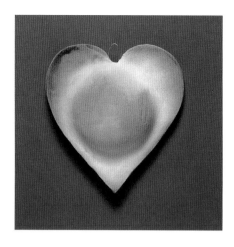

window, open the door regularly to check.) Remove the dough as soon as it has reached the desired shade. Avoid leaving your project too long—a very deep brown could turn black in seconds, burning your dough or making it too brittle to use. Allow the dough to cool completely before painting and/or varnishing.

Browning will deepen a project's base shade, providing a rich background for paint finishes. Use it as a coloring process on its own, or add a little spot-color (see the Molded Heart above and on pages 68–9, the African Dolls, pages 70–5, or the Wheat Plaque, pages 94–5). Subtle shade changes produced by allowing the dough to blush naturally will give your work a dramatic finish, especially if you apply several coats of gloss varnish to deepen and enrich the dough's color still further.

AIR DRYING

Although it takes longer (days and weeks, rather than hours), air drying saves on fuel bills and does not monopolize the oven. Again, exact drying times depend on the size and thickness

of the project and the surrounding temperature and humidity. Objects must be left undisturbed on a flat surface in a dry place—an open cupboard is ideal. The temperature should be constant, but still keep a close eye on your dough since it may warp slightly.

On warm summer days, thinner objects can be dried outside, and if you are lucky enough to live in a warm climate all year round, a shed or garage could be a perfect drying environment.

Dough should never be exposed to damp or extreme changes in temperature (see Preserving your Work).

FILLING AND REPAIRING

Small hairline cracks in raw dough caused by bending and molding, for example, can be repaired as and when they happen. Paint a little standard watery dough paste on the crack to seal it and continue modeling the dough.

Cracks sometimes appear as the dough starts to harden and dry. This can happen before or during baking. Heat is an excellent sealant, so repairing your dough while it is still warm (not hot) from the oven is often very successful. To fill hairline cracks, brush standard watery dough paste over the crack while the dough is still warm. The warmth from the dough should seal the crack quickly. Hairline cracks which appear after baking when the dough has cooled down should be sealed with a thicker paste.

To fill larger cracks, brush thicker dough paste into the crack (taking care not to press too hard) and then level-off any surface bumps by brushing a light coating of paste over the affected area. Brush on a little water to smooth out the paste. If necessary, return the object to the oven for a few minutes to seal. When the paste has hardened (and the dough is cool) run your finger over the repair. If the surface is rough, rub over lightly with fine sandpaper before painting your model.

Where salt dough is built up in layers (cutouts, petals, or shells on a base, for example) any unsightly gaps and joints which appear after baking should be sealed and smoothed over with thickened dough paste. Smooth over as before. After repairing, return the object to the oven. If you are still worried about the strength of a joint, wait until the object is cool and use a little craft glue.

PAINTING

The paint finishes in this book are meant to supply you with ideas, not hard-and-fast rules. The easiest way to adapt any of the projects is to change the colors that appear in the photographs. If, for example, you prefer the idea of gold highlights on a black, rather than a red background, use the information on highlighting to guide you and apply your own choice of color.

If you can't commit yourself to a color scheme right away, make a rough drawing of the object and experiment on paper first. To get an idea of the way certain colors (and thicknesses) of paint react to salt dough, roll out raw dough to a thickness of $3/8$ in., cut into squares, and bake. When these tiles of dough have cooled, use them to experiment with color and paint effects. You could also varnish your painted tile to see how colors intensify under a glossy

surface. When you start painting the dough, be decisive. Water-based paints dry very quickly, so use bold brush strokes on large areas and paint evenly. Never overload your brush— the moisture could seep down into the salt dough.

Try restricting yourself to a certain number of colors (the choice is yours), but keep a couple in reserve to create contrast between textures.

Some objects lend themselves to groups of colors, but this need not be restricting. A simple leaf can be painted in shades of green, yellow, purple, brown, red, gold, and burnt orange.

Use darker shades of the same color for definition—a deeper green on the veins of leaves, for example.

Tubes of watercolors and acrylics are easily mixed and diluted and are therefore excellent for varying color density. (Avoid oil-based products.)

PAINTING MATERIALS
Paints—a good range of watercolors, acrylics, or other water-based paints
Brushes—buy the best you can—four or five, ranging from a thicker brush for stroking on large areas of background color to a fine-haired brush for detail (Cheaper brushes can be used, but only if their bristles are soft and firmly attached)
Cotton swabs—for blotting excess moisture
Soft, lint-free rags or kitchen towel—for applying paint effects

PAINT TECHNIQUES
Color washes
Applied in layers to build up color gradually, color washes create a gentle, finely-blended effect. They can also be used as subtle background colors, or as

thin overlays (to tone down stronger base colors). Washes are simply diluted paints, brushed over areas in sweeping strokes. Mix paint with water until it is fluid and loose enough to wash over the surface of the dough, leaving an even tint of color.

Although washes are very watery, their colors should not be insipid. Judge the amount of water needed by adding enough to produce the desired shade.

Gold or silver washes are very effective when applied over other colors. Brushed over strong base coats, they produce a luxurious, even sheen and provide glimpses of the color beneath (see the Molded Stars below and on pages 42–3).

Dabbing on

The term dabbing on is used to describe the way patches of color are applied as contrasts to base colors. Dabbing, rather than painting or brushing on color, produces a natural, soft-edged effect—this makes it ideal for "organic" decorations like leaves and fruits. Use a soft rag, a piece of paper towel, or even your finger to dab a small amount of contrasting paint onto the dough. If necessary, dab off any excess paint with a clean piece of

rag or paper towel. The fruits on the Christmas Wreath (above and on pages 91–3) and in the Traditional Fruit Basket (pages 36–7) are painted and then dabbed with darker and lighter colors for contrast.

Brushing on highlights

Highlights draw attention to areas of texture or color. The cornflowers on the Wheat Plaque (pages 94–5) have been highlighted in blue. A highlight can be any color that accents or complements the base. Gold and silver add a subtle sheen to decorations—but the trick is to know when to stop. Too many highlights can swamp a design, so be selective about the areas you treat.

Apply a tiny amount of gold paint with an almost-dry paintbrush. Stroke your brush over the chosen area and wipe over quickly with a piece of paper towel to leave slivers of highlights. (Highlights can also be dabbed on with a soft rag, or with your finger.)

Toning down and blending

Water-based paint dries quickly, which can prove a problem if you are unsure about the finish you have produced. However, as long as you know how to tone colors down and blend edges, minor mistakes need not be a problem.

If a color wash looks too pale or insipid, simply apply more washes until you are happy with the result.

A dark color can often be muted by washing over with a lighter, complementary shade. Or, tone down a color by brushing on a little water and dabbing immediately with a clean rag while the paint is still damp (this should lift off some of the paint).

If painting produces a hard-edged finish, apply a complementary color wash (or apply plain water). Gently dab at any hard-definition lines with a cotton swab or small piece of rag to blend and soften the effect.

Burnishing

A "polishing" technique, burnishing produces a muted, antique effect. This finish gives glittering colors like gold a more subtle sheen (see Molded Sun, pages 46–7). You must work quickly, since the base coat should still be damp when you apply the burnish. With a soft rag, a paper towel, or your finger, dab tiny amounts of black paint (diluted with water) over a (still-damp) gold-painted area. Before the black paint is completely dry, rub with a soft rag (using small, circular polishing movements).

This technique was used on the Gift for a New Baby shown above and on pages 126–7.

VARNISHING

Not only does it help to seal and protect your work, varnish also adds a veneer of depth and richness to surface colors and brings out the natural tones of baked but unpainted salt dough. Careless varnishing can ruin a beautifully-painted object, so apply each coat carefully, using a smaller brush for fine-relief and decorative areas. You can use spray varnish if you wish.

Whether you use gloss or matte varnish is up to you. Some people prefer a high-definition shine on everything, while others go for a more subtle effect. The projects in this book are finished with gloss polyurethane varnish, but a matte finish can be just as effective.

- Cover a flat surface with newspaper (to protect it).
- Apply each coat carefully, using even strokes and enough varnish to cover the surface evenly. If the varnish drips off the brush, you are using too much.
- Each object will need five or six coats of varnish.
- Varnish the backs of projects to seal and protect them.
- Let each coat dry completely before applying the next.
- When varnishing more than one object at a time, make a simple chart to record the number of coats applied to each.
- Always clean brushes thoroughly after use.

Egg white is a natural-looking varnish for traditional, unpainted salt dough objects (like wreaths). Brush the egg white on before baking. This finish is not so long-lasting as chemical varnish.

Varnishing tools
- Paintbrushes (a nylon-bristle brush is suitable, but do check that the bristles are firmly attached)
- Stir stick (to stir varnish)
- Polyurethane varnish—clear gloss or clear matte (You can use acrylic varnish if you wish.)
- Turpentine (for cleaning brushes)

FINISHING YOUR WORK
Painting and varnishing the backs of finished pieces will protect your models, but if you're worried about filled cracks, general repairs, or an uneven finish, you may prefer to cover the backs of plaques, frames, mirrors, and some decorations. Use (thin) cork tiles as backing. Cut cork to size and glue into place. Felt makes a good backing; again, cut to size and glue. Or, try a short cut and use adhesive-backed felt that can be peeled and stuck into place.

PRESERVING YOUR WORK
Although it is surprisingly strong and long-lasting, salt dough is also extremely susceptible to changes in temperature and humidity. Varnishing your work carefully will help to seal and protect it, but you should avoid damp atmospheres like bathrooms and steamy kitchens (or areas in kitchens that become steamy—around ranges and counters where a kettle is in use). Never display salt dough in rooms where the temperature fluctuates from one extreme to another (for example, sunrooms, storm porches, or unheated greenhouses). Avoid placing salt dough too near radiators or heaters. Window ledges may seem ideal places to display your work, but they can become very cold and damp.

SAFETY
There is a very real danger of children mistaking salt dough for cakes or cookies and this can be especially hazardous where crafts contain wires. Make sure that finished decorations and hanging plaques are kept well out of reach. Keep lids on varnish and sharper tools out of reach. Take normal safety precautions when baking.

Nature's Gifts

The fresh colors of spring, the brilliance of summer, the
rich hues of fall or the cool shades of winter—whatever the
season, nature provides the inspiration for these designs.
The simplest images are often the most effective.
Sometimes, just the shape of a leaf or the color of a plant
will spark an idea.
Although the salt dough projects in this section are easy to
reproduce exactly, they are also designed to provide you
with ideas and inspiration. Vary the sizes and shapes of the
individual pieces, or add some personal touches to give your
work a truly original finish.

LEAF DISHES

These dishes are designed to be practical and decorative. Fill them with candy or cookies for special occasions, or use them as potpourri holders. Once you have mastered the art of working on a mold, you can re-create your favorite leaf shapes by adapting our instructions. Either cut your leaf freehand or vary the size of the templates provided to make a larger or smaller dish. Nothing could be more simple and dramatic than the shape and colors of a leaf, especially if you choose deep, rich shades. Brush washes of diluted paint over your dish to build up a natural-looking surface finish, then highlight the leaf's shape and texture by dabbing on deeper colors.

Before beginning, please read "Materials and Techniques," pp. 10–21.

MATERIALS AND EQUIPMENT

Salt dough (see page 12)
Dough paste (see page 13)
Nonstick baking sheet
Rolling pin
Leaf template (page 130)
Small kitchen knife
Small wooden spatula
Ovenproof dish (about 6½ in.
in diameter)
Aluminum foil
Pastry brush
Paintbrushes for applying dough paste,
paints, and varnish
Rag or paper towel to apply paint finishes
Orange and brown water-based paints
Gloss polyurethane varnish

1 Cover the outside of the ovenproof bowl with foil, folding about 2 in. of the foil over the lip of the bowl. Flatten the foil until it is smooth all over. Roll out the dough to a thickness of about ¼ in. Lay the template on the dough and cut around it to make the leaf shape.

2 Lift the dough leaf carefully and lay it over the upside-down, foil-covered bowl. Smooth with a damp (not wet) pastry brush, taking care not to stretch the dough out of shape as you do so. Pat and smooth any rough edges with the spatula or damp pastry brush. Using the small kitchen knife, score the veins onto the leaf. Indent the edge of the leaf at the end of each vein for a scalloped effect.

3 Bake until the surface is dry-looking and hard enough to handle without distorting. Remove the ovenproof bowl and carefully peel the foil away. Place the dough leaf dish right side up on the baking sheet and return it to the oven to finish baking.

4 Paint the dish with a wash of brown paint. Don't worry about surface cracks—the paint will sink into them, adding to the veined effect. Now dilute some orange paint with a little water. Dip a soft rag into the paint and dab it over the leaf. When the paint is dry, varnish your dish.

GRAPEVINE BASKET

Although it looks elaborate, this basket is surprisingly easy to make. As long as you weave a good, strong lattice surface and flatten it out evenly, attaching the vine leaves and grapes could not be simpler.

Don't let size restrict you; the basket pictured here was molded on a 7 in. ovenproof bowl, but smaller or larger bowls are just as effective. Although it is easier to cut out and score more than one leaf at a time, take care to cover any shapes that are not in immediate use with a cloth, to prevent them from drying out. The basket's decorative leaves and grapes should look lush and natural; drape the grapes in succulent bunches. Lift, twist, and overlap the edges of the vine leaves, arranging some at angles and curving others over the lip of the basket. Then paint your bowl in rich shades and brush or dab on contrasting colors for a sumptuous finish. Alternatively, you could brown your bowl and just paint the leaves and fruit, as for the bowl on the right on pages 23. When the paint is completely dry, apply several coats of gloss varnish. Allow each coat to dry thoroughly before applying the next and the result will be a deep, long-lasting sheen.

Before beginning, please read "Materials and Techniques," pp. 10–21.

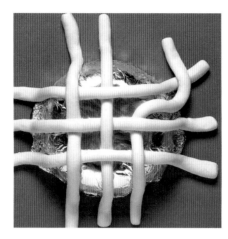

1 Cover the outside of the ovenproof bowl with foil, folding about 2 in. of foil over the lip of the bowl. Smooth the foil all over. Roll sausage-shaped dough strips by hand; the strips should be a little longer than the distance from rim to rim of the upside-down bowl. Although you will eventually flatten the dough strips with a rolling pin, try to roll each strip to an even thickness of about $^{3}/_{8}$ in. Roll a few strips at a time and cover the rest of your dough to prevent its drying out.

2 Start weaving your bowl by positioning a cross of two strips in the center of the upside-down bowl. Now add more strips, weaving them over and under as you go. Make the gaps between your latticework as even as possible. These strips will spread when they are flattened, so leave enough space between them as you weave.

3 Once the bowl is covered with woven strips, lightly roll over the whole area with a rolling pin (this will give you an even surface for decoration). The strips should now be flattened to a thickness of about $^{1}/_{4}$ in. Trim any excess dough away from the rim, and gently squeeze the overlapping edges of the pieces so that they stick neatly together.

4 Roll an edging strip by hand, to go around the circumference of the bowl. This edging strip will cover any untidy ends. Press it lightly into place, or attach it with a little dough paste.

5 To make the grapes, roll oval balls of dough about $^{3}/_{8}$ in. long. Arrange the balls in bunch shapes. Position a bunch of grapes on every other vertical lattice strip (below the edging strip). Attach with dough paste. Next, gently flatten the edging strip by hand.

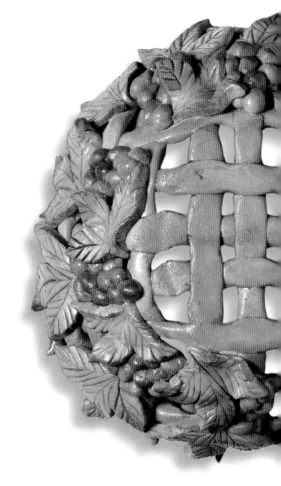

6 To make vine leaves, roll out dough to a thickness of about ¼ in. Cut around leaf template. With your knife, score veins on the leaf. Repeat. Arrange leaves around the edge of the bowl, overlapping some and twisting the tips of others to make them look natural. Attach with dough paste. Arrange more leaves around the outside of the bowl; attach with dough paste. Bake the upside-down bowl.

7 When the bowl is hard enough to handle without distorting, take it from the oven, remove the ovenproof bowl, and peel away the foil. Return the dough bowl, right side up, to the oven until the bowl and leaves are baked through. When cool, apply a wash of dark green paint to the inside of the bowl, and when this is dry, turn the bowl over and paint the lattice part of the bowl in the same color.

8 Paint the leaves with a wash of light green paint. While the wash is still damp, dab on a little brown or dark green paint with a brush or soft rag. Paint a purple wash over the grapes. Before the wash is dry, dab on a little brown or darker paint for contrast. When dry, varnish.

MATERIALS AND EQUIPMENT

Salt dough (see page 12)
Dough paste (see page 13)
Nonstick baking sheet
Rolling pin
Vine leaf template (page 130)
Small kitchen knife
Small wooden spatula
Ovenproof bowl (about 7 in. in diameter)
Aluminum foil
Pastry brush
Paintbrushes for applying dough paste,
paints, and varnish
Rag or paper towel to apply paint finishes
Light green, dark green, brown, and purple
water-based paints
Gloss polyurethane varnish

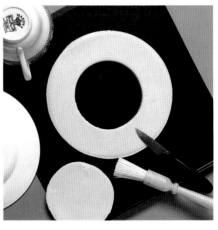

1 Working directly on the baking sheet, roll out dough to a thickness of about $1/4$ in. Lay the plate on top of the dough and cut around it. Now stamp a hole in the center by pressing down on the cup or glass. Try to make the dough area of the ring about 2 in. across. Tidy any rough edges and smooth the surface with a damp pastry brush.

2 To make sunflower centers, roll a ball of dough, flatten it with your thumb, and position it on your wreath. Do this four times, arranging the centers at equal intervals around the wreath. Attach with dough paste.

SUNFLOWER WREATH

This sunflower wreath uses strong colors and varied textures to make a bright impression. Follow the instructions to create your wreath base and sunflowers then, using the template, make and attach the leaves. Use dried cloves to give the sunflower centers a natural finish—other dried spices, small beads, or balls of painted salt dough are good alternatives. You may prefer the subtle tones of baked dough to the bright colors used here. If so, wait until the leaves and petals become a deeper shade of gold, then let the wreath cool down before sealing it with varnish for a deep lasting sheen.

Before beginning, please read "Materials and Techniques," pp. 10–21.

3 To make petals, roll small balls of dough between your palms, flatten, and shape them into ovals (about ⅜ in. long and ¼ in. thick). Arrange petals around each sunflower center; attach with dough paste. Score lines on petals with the knife.

4 Push dried cloves (flower end up) into the sunflower centers. To make the leaves, roll out dough to a thickness of about ¼ in. and cut out around the template. Using the photograph as a guide, arrange the leaves. Twist and overlap some of the leaves to make them look natural. Attach with dough paste. Score veins on leaves with the knife.

MATERIALS AND EQUIPMENT

Salt dough (see page 12)
Dough paste (see page 13)
Nonstick baking sheet
Rolling pin
Small leaf template (page 131)
Small kitchen knife
Small wooden spatula
Pastry brush
Plate to cut around for wreath shape (about 8 in. in diameter)
Cup or glass to stamp out central hole (about 4 in. in diameter)
Cloves for decoration
Paintbrushes for applying dough paste, paints, and varnish
Rag or paper towel to apply paint finishes
Yellow, green, brown, and black water-based paints
Gloss polyurethane varnish

5 Bake your wreath. When cool, paint the base shape of the wreath with diluted brown paint. Cover the leaves with a wash of green paint, and with a soft rag dab on a little black paint for a natural effect. Paint the sunflower petals a vibrant yellow and leave the centers their natural dough color. When the paint is dry, varnish the sunflower wreath.

BEE AND FLOWER MOBILE

Although it is not designed to spin and flutter in the breeze, this bee and flower mobile should sway gently when touched. Hang it near a window or a lamp, and the light will make the colors even more vibrant. The photographs are here to guide you, and you can introduce your own ideas and finishing touches to produce a very original finish. Add more beads and bells, or use small cookie cutters to make tiny dough shapes for threading. To copy the mobile exactly, you should make two large flowers, two medium flowers, and two small ones. All the flowers are made in exactly the same way. As long as you calculate the right amount of wire for the finished mobile, you can thread on as many decorations as you like.

Before beginning, please read "Materials and Techniques," pp. 10–21.

MATERIALS AND EQUIPMENT

Salt dough (see page 12)
Dough paste (see page 13)
Nonstick baking sheet
Rolling pin
Ruler
Small kitchen knife
Small wooden spatula
Pastry brush
18-gauge wire, about 2¼ yds.
Wire cutters
Round-ended pliers
Beads, bell for decoration
Paintbrushes for applying dough paste,
paints, and varnish
Rag or paper towel to apply paint finishes
Water-based paints
Gloss polyurethane varnish

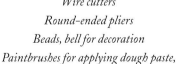

1 Roll a ball of dough between your palms. Working directly on the baking sheet (so that the flowers' backs are flattened), flatten the ball gently with your thumb or palm. Indent the center by pressing down with your thumb or forefinger. Using the blunt edge of the knife, score indentations to make petal sections, and a small circle to form the center of the flower. If necessary, go over each indentation a second time to make good, strong dividing lines. Complete the flower by rolling a small ball of dough and attaching it to the flower shape with dough paste. Make two large flowers about 1½ in. across, two medium flowers about 1¼ in. across, and two small ones about 1 in. across. Each flower is about ⅜ in. thick when flattened out.

2 Working directly on the baking sheet, make four leaves about 1½ in. long and about ¾ in. across: Roll out dough to a thickness of about ⅜ in. and cut out leaf shapes with the knife. Score in veins. Now make two larger leaves about 2½ in. long and ⅜ in. thick. Press them together (a little dough paste may help). Attach one of the large flowers to the middle of this leaf shape.

3 Working directly on the baking sheet (so that the bees have flat backs), roll balls of dough about ¾ x ¾ in. and about ⅜ in. thick). Roll smaller balls of dough; shape them into wings and attach two to each ball-shaped bee. Make six bees.

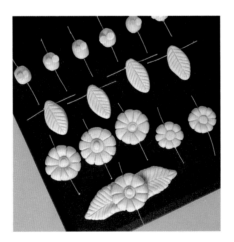

4 Guide a piece of 3¼ in. wire through the middle of each flower and bee shape. Thread wires through the top of each leaf shape. Leave enough wire jutting out at each edge of each shape to turn during baking. Bake, rotating the wires occasionally to keep the holes open.

5 When cool, paint each piece according to the photograph, or paint as you wish. (Hold each dough piece by its wire to make painting easier.) When the paint is dry, varnish the dough pieces. When the varnish is dry, remove the wires carefully.

6 To calculate the length of wire for vertical threading, lay all the shapes in the correct order on a flat surface. Leave space in between for beads. Measure the total length of shapes and beads (about 13 in. if you're following the measurements exactly). Add an extra 2½ in. for a hanging loop at the top and an extra 1¼ in. at the bottom for the bell and locking loop. Cut the wire with the wire cutters.

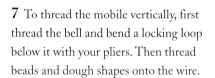

7 To thread the mobile vertically, first thread the bell and bend a locking loop below it with your pliers. Then thread beads and dough shapes onto the wire.

8 Calculate the length of wire for the horizontal part of the mobile in the same way as you did for the vertical threading. Cut the correct length of wire. Before threading your shapes, twist the center of the (horizontal) wire around the wire remaining at the top of the vertical piece. Turn the wire a couple of times, making sure that some still remains jutting up from the vertical. Now thread shapes along the right and left of the horizontal wire. When you've finished threading, bend locking loops at each end of the horizontal part of your mobile. Twist the remaining wire at the top of the mobile into a hanging loop.

MATERIALS AND EQUIPMENT
Salt dough (see page 12)
Dough paste (see page 13)
Nonstick baking sheet
Rolling pin
Basket and small leaf templates (page 131)
Small kitchen knife
Small wooden spatula
Garlic press
Pastry brush
Cloves for decoration
Paintbrushes for applying dough paste,
paints, and varnish
Rag or paper towel to apply paint finishes
Water-based paints
Gloss polyurethane varnish

TRADITIONAL FRUIT BASKET

Piled high with delicious-looking fruit, this traditional basket brims with nature's harvest. Size need not restrict you—if you would like to make a larger or smaller basket, enlarge or reduce the size of the template accordingly. Once you have cut out the base shape and added the decorative wickerwork, you can alter the arrangement and contents of the basket to suit your own taste or even the season of the year. The overall impression should be full-blown and luxurious, so brush on touches of contrasting color to give the fruit a ripening blush.

Before beginning, please read "Materials and Techniques," pp. 10–21. Work directly on the baking sheet.

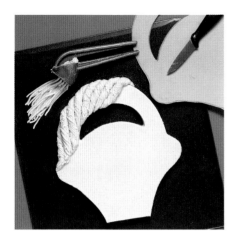

1 Roll out dough to a thickness of about $^3/_8$ in. Cut around the template; smooth and tidy any rough edges with the spatula. Squeeze balls of dough through the garlic press. Twist each bunch of squeezed strands twice, and arrange on the handle.

2 Now make a rim for the basket, using the same method. But this time, lay the twisted strands end to end. Use a little dough paste to attach all the strands. The rim defines the area above which you will lay the fruit.

3 With the blade of the knife, score a woven effect onto the basket. Work down the basket scoring straight, horizontal lines. Then score diagonal lines across the basket, from left to right and another series of lines from right to left.

4 Roll out more dough, this time to a thickness of $^1/_4$ in. Cut around the leaf template to make nine leaves; tidy any rough edges. Score in veins. Arrange two groups of three leaves and attach one group to the right and the other to the left-hand corner of the basket. Twist the tips of the leaves to make them look natural. Now attach another group of three leaves at the top center of the basket (see photograph).

5 The oranges and apples are simply balls of dough, about $1^1/_4$ in. across. Arrange and attach them to the basket shape. Press dried cloves into the fruit, flower side up for the oranges and stalk side up for the apples. You will eventually paint these balls of dough their appropriate colors.

6 The grapes are smaller balls of dough, arranged in bunches. Tease the ends of dough balls into points to make plums. The nuts are smaller, round balls of dough. Arrange and attach the plums, grapes, and nuts. Cut single leaves out of dough and use them to fill any gaps in your fruit arrangement. Attach them with dough paste and score in veins. Bake, remove from oven. When cool, paint referring to the photograph. When dry, varnish.

1 Working directly on the baking sheet, roll out the dough to a thickness of about ³/₈ in. Place the templates on top of the dough and cut carefully around each shape. Smooth and tidy any rough edges with the spatula or damp pastry brush.

MATERIALS AND EQUIPMENT

Salt dough (see page 12)
Dough paste (see page 13)
Nonstick baking sheet
Bird and heart templates (page 131)
Rolling pin
Ruler
Small kitchen knife
Small wooden spatula
Pastry brush
18-gauge wire, about 13¹/₂ in.
Wire cutters
Round-ended pliers
Beads, bell for decoration
Paintbrushes for applying dough paste,
paints, and varnish
Water-based paints
Gloss polyurethane varnish

BIRD HANGING

Simple shapes are often the most rewarding to decorate. You can transform dough cutouts just by painting them in spectacular colors and adding delicate patterns. This bird hanging is also a good way of displaying beads or fancy buttons. Or why not make your own beads? Simply roll small balls of dough, pierce them with wire, and then rotate the wires to keep the holes open during baking. Paint the beads in bright, jewel-like colors. The result is an original hanging, decorated with individual style.

Before beginning, please read "Materials and Techniques," pp. 10–21.

2 Attach the wing to the body of the bird, sealing the edges with a small amount of dough paste. With the knife, gently score a dividing line between the bird's beak and head. Indent the eye shape with the end of a paintbrush.

3 Keeping the wire parallel to the baking sheet and taking care not to distort the dough, carefully guide a 3½ in. length of wire through the bird's body. Then guide a 2½ in. length of wire through the dough heart. Bake, rotating the wires about every 15 minutes to keep the holes open.

4 When baked, allow the pieces to cool and then use your round-ended pliers to withdraw the wires. Paint the bird and heart, (and your beads) using the photographs as a guide. When dry, varnish.

5 To calculate the length of wire for final threading, lay the bird, beads, heart, and bell on a flat surface. Allow enough wire for bending into a hanging loop at the top and a smaller, locking loop at the bottom, then cut the wire to the correct length. Bend a tight, locking loop at the bottom and thread the bell, heart, beads, and bird onto the wire. Shape the top of the wire into a hanging loop.

Essential Elements

The sea and the sky are limitless sources of inspiration. Whether you are making something as ethereal as a star, or simply trying to model a seashell by hand—remember that the unexpected can produce interesting results, so don't strive too hard for perfection.

The designs that follow use molding, hand modeling, and decorative relief work to produce very original finishes. The instructions show you how to lift flat shapes into new dimensions simply by mastering a few, basic skills. Spectacular paint effects are just as easy, so let the elements inspire you to produce touches of pure fantasy.

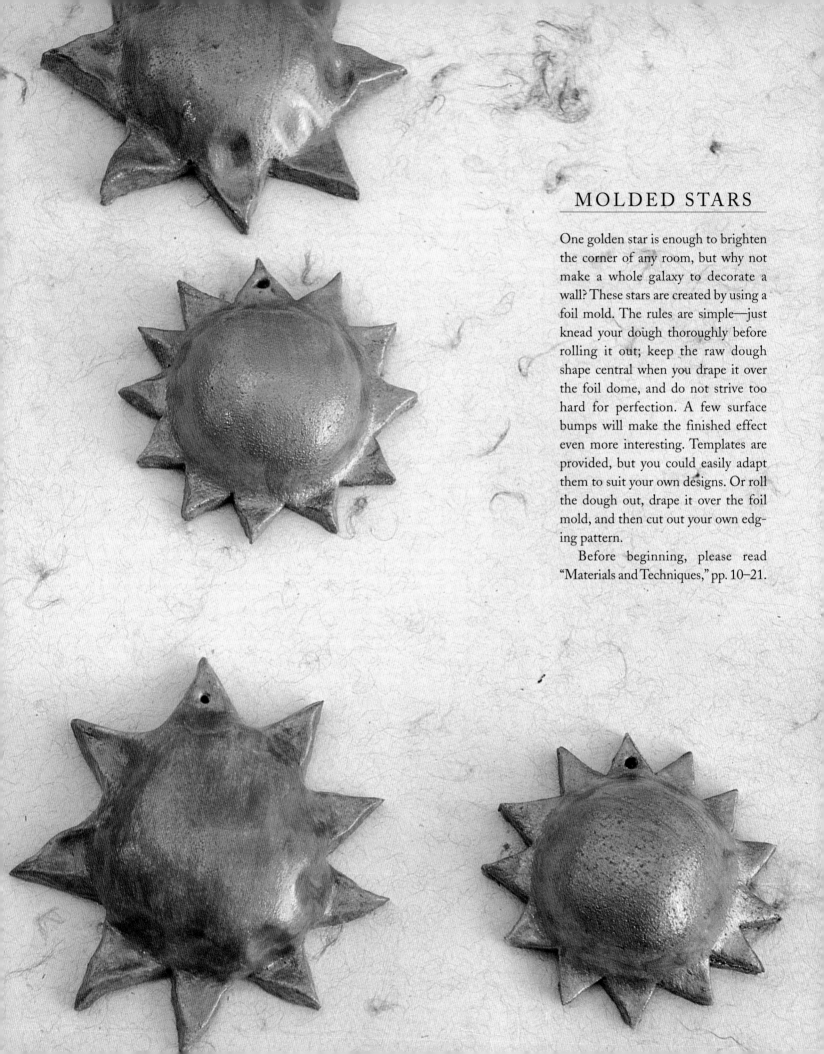

MOLDED STARS

One golden star is enough to brighten the corner of any room, but why not make a whole galaxy to decorate a wall? These stars are created by using a foil mold. The rules are simple—just knead your dough thoroughly before rolling it out; keep the raw dough shape central when you drape it over the foil dome, and do not strive too hard for perfection. A few surface bumps will make the finished effect even more interesting. Templates are provided, but you could easily adapt them to suit your own designs. Or roll the dough out, drape it over the foil mold, and then cut out your own edging pattern.

Before beginning, please read "Materials and Techniques," pp. 10–21.

MATERIALS AND EQUIPMENT

Salt dough (see page 12)
Dough paste (see page 13)
Nonstick baking sheet
Rolling pin
Star template (page 132)
Small kitchen knife
Small wooden spatula
Aluminum foil
Pastry brush
Spatula
Paintbrushes for applying dough paste,
paints, and varnish
Rag or paper towel to apply paint finishes
Orange and gold water-based paints
Gloss polyurethane varnish

1 Working directly on the baking sheet, roll the dough out to a thickness of about $1/4$ in. Lay the template on top of the dough and cut around the shape carefully.

2 Roll some foil between your palms to make a ball. Flatten one side of the foil to make a dome shape; the dome should measure about $2\frac{1}{2}$ in. across the base and be about 1 in. high.

Use the template provided or vary the star design by draping the dough over the foil mold and cut out the rays freehand, as pictured above.

3 Place the foil mold on the baking sheet. Lay the dough on top of the dome, taking care to center it. Gently pat and flatten the star's rays on the baking sheet. Use the end of a paintbrush to pierce a hanging hole in one of the rays. Smooth any rough edges with a damp pastry brush or a spatula. Half-bake, remove the foil mold, and return to the oven to finish baking.

4 Allow to cool. Either use gold paint, or apply an orange paint as a base, followed by a wash of gold. When the paint is completely dry, varnish.

MOLDED SUN

A burnished-gold paint finish gives this sun a luxurious sheen. Its contours gleam in daylight and glow mysteriously under artificial light. Molded on foil in exactly the same way as the stars on pages 42–3, the sun is larger, so the dough is thicker and the rays are longer. Blend the features into the base shape, but bear in mind that hand modeling is not an exact process. If you want to vary the shape and facial expression, go ahead. Make the rays eye-catching; surface ripples and waves look very effective, especially when they are painted and varnished, so be as adventurous as you can.

Before beginning, please read "Materials and Techniques," pp. 10–21.

1 Working directly on the baking sheet, roll dough out to about ³⁄₈ in. Lay the template on top of the dough and cut around the shape.

2 When the dough is on its foil mold, vary the shape of the sun's rays by squeezing and shaping them between your thumb and forefinger until they become uneven and wavy. Taking care not to distort the dough, score lines down the rays.

MATERIALS AND EQUIPMENT
Salt dough (see page 12)
Dough paste (see page 13)
Nonstick baking sheet
Rolling pin
Sun template (pages 132–3)
Small kitchen knife
Small wooden spatula
Aluminum foil
Pastry brush
Spatula
Paintbrushes for applying dough paste, paints, and varnish
Rag or paper towel to apply paint finishes
Gold and black water-based paints
Gloss polyurethane varnish

3 Roll out four small sausage shapes for the eyebrows and eyelids, two sausage shapes for the lips, and a slightly thicker sausage for the nose. Roll two small balls for the nostrils and two small, flattened balls for the eyes. Position the features and attach them with a little dough paste. Shape and blend the nostrils into the end of the nose, and indent the underside of nostrils with the end of a paintbrush.

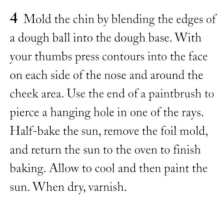

4 Mold the chin by blending the edges of a dough ball into the dough base. With your thumbs press contours into the face on each side of the nose and around the cheek area. Use the end of a paintbrush to pierce a hanging hole in one of the rays. Half-bake the sun, remove the foil mold, and return the sun to the oven to finish baking. Allow to cool and then paint the sun. When dry, varnish.

To paint, apply a thin wash of gold paint. While the paint is still damp, dab on a little black paint. Rub off in small, circular movements for a mottled effect.

MOLDED MOON

Shimmering color washes will add a supernatural touch to this salt dough moon, especially if the surface is rippled and uneven.

Once you have draped the raw dough over your foil mold, gently squeeze the moon into a crescent shape by hand. Your fingers will pucker the dough as you squeeze, automatically producing the right effect. Then use your thumbs to indent the surface. Blend the moon's features into the dough shape carefully and take care when baking (heavily-contoured shapes can easily overcook). Try to keep the underside level at all times, but don't worry if the finished moon doesn't hang absolutely flat against the wall. Any shadows that it casts will simply add to the three-dimensional effect.

Before beginning, please read "Materials and Techniques," pp. 10–21.

1 Make a crescent-shaped foil mold measuring approximately $8\frac{1}{2}$ in. in length and $3\frac{1}{4}$ in. at the widest point. Place the mold on the baking sheet.

2 Roll dough out to about $\frac{3}{8}$ in. and carefully lay it over the foil mold. Cut around the mold and smooth any rough edges with the spatula or damp pastry brush. Add interest and surface contours to the basic moon shape by gently squeezing to distort it. Pucker the surface by pressing in contours with your thumbs. Make an indentation for the mouth.

3 To model the moon's face, roll a cone-shaped piece of dough for the nose and flatten the underside. Attach the nose to the moon with a little dough paste and blend the edges into the overall shape. Roll two dough sausages for the eyebrow and eyelid. Curl and attach them to the moon, using a little dough paste.

4 Roll a ball for the eye, flatten it, and attach with dough paste. Indent the eye with the end of a paintbrush. Roll out a piece of dough about $\frac{1}{8}$ in. thick. Use the glass or a jar lid to stamp out a circle for the cheek. Attach with dough paste. Half-bake the moon, remove the foil, and return to the oven to finish baking.

MATERIALS AND EQUIPMENT

Salt dough (see page 12)
Dough paste (see page 13)
Nonstick baking sheet
Ruler
Rolling pin
Small kitchen knife
Small wooden spatula
Aluminum foil
Pastry brush
Lid or glass to stamp out cheek circle (about
2 in. in diameter)
Spatula
Paintbrushes for applying dough paste,
paints, and varnish
Rag or paper towel to apply paint finishes
Blue, silver, and black water-based paints
Gloss polyurethane varnish

To paint the moon, apply a thin wash of blue paint. While the blue paint is still damp, cover with a wash of silver paint. Using a soft rag or paper towel, blend both colors together while still damp. Next, dab on tiny amounts of black paint. Rub off in small, circular movements. When the paint is completely dry, varnish.

MERMAID MIRROR

This mirror makes a perfect gift for those fascinated by the mystery of the sea. As long as you preheat your oven to a low setting and let the dough cool down in the oven after baking, this project can be baked with the mirror embedded into it. And because the edges of the mirror will be hidden by a rolled-dough frame, you could use a piece of broken mirror instead of a brand new one. To convey the impression of shimmering sea water, brush washes of green paint onto the base of the plaque and then rub over with gold. Emphasize the relief work on the mirror by coloring the mermaids in contrasting shades, and burnish with highlights of gold.

Before beginning, please read "Materials and Techniques," pp. 10–21.

MATERIALS AND EQUIPMENT

Salt dough (see page 12)

Dough paste (see page 13)

Nonstick baking sheet

Rolling pin

Ruler

Mermaid template (page 133)

Small kitchen knife

Small wooden spatula

Pocket-sized mirror (about 2½ in. wide and ⅛ in. thick)

Garlic press

Pastry brush

Paintbrushes for applying dough paste, paints, and varnish

Greens, gold, and other desired colors of water-based paints

Gloss polyurethane varnish

1 Work directly on the baking sheet. Roll out dough to a thickness of about ¼ in. Using the ruler and knife, cut out a rectangle about 5½ x 7½ in. Tidy any rough edges with the spatula or the damp pastry brush. Now score a border about ¼ in. in from the edge of the dough rectangle.

2 Center the mirror in the top half of the rectangle with the lower edge of the mirror about 4¼ in. above the bottom. Press the mirror into the dough gently (don't press too hard, or you will distort the dough).

3 Roll a sausage of dough (about ⅜ in. thick) by hand. Attach the sausage around the mirror with dough paste. Make sure that it is firmly attached and sealed along its edges. Score the inner edge and make indentations all the way around the frame with the end of a paintbrush.

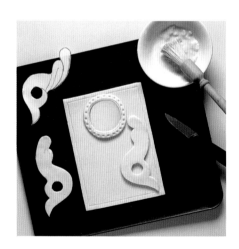

4 Roll out dough to a thickness of about ¼ in. Cut around the mermaid template. Tidy any rough edges with the spatula or damp pastry brush and put this dough shape aside. Now turn the template over and cut around it to make another mermaid in reverse. Tidy any rough edges. Using the photograph as a guide, arrange the mermaids below the mirror and attach them with dough paste.

5 To make the mermaids' hair, push balls of dough through a garlic press. Arrange and attach these strands, using the photograph as a guide. To make the arms, roll two sausages of dough (about 2¼ in. long and ⅜ in. across) and position one on each mermaid. Using a damp paintbrush, press and blend the edges into the bodies of the mermaids.

6 Score a line across each body to define the start of the tail. To give the impression of scales, make indentations all over each mermaid's tail using the end of a paintbrush. Bake in a preheated oven at the coolest setting. When the dough is baked, turn off oven and leave dough inside the oven to cool down. Paint, following the photograph. Varnish.

SHELL BOX

This container is perfect for storing loose beads, small buttons, a collection of shells, or anything that is too precious to leave lying around.

When you have constructed the basic box shape, refer to page 14 for instructions on hand-modeling the decorative shells. Then arrange the shells in natural-looking groups for a finish that is realistic enough to have been swept ashore by the sea.

A wash of orange paint will produce a warm, pearly effect. Dab tiny amounts of black paint onto small areas, then rub off immediately, leaving subtle highlights.

Unpainted baked dough can be extremely effective too. Carefully brown the dough in the oven. When the shells have flushed a deeper shade, remove the box and let it cool down. Finally, apply several coats of gloss varnish to give the shell box a rich, lustrous sheen.

Before beginning, please read "Materials and Techniques," pp. 10–21.

MATERIALS AND EQUIPMENT

Salt dough (see page 12)
Dough paste (see page 13)
Nonstick baking sheet
Rolling pin
Ruler
Stiff cardboard
Adhesive tape
Small kitchen knife
Aluminum foil
Pastry brush
Paintbrushes for applying dough paste, paints, and varnish
Orange and black water-based paints
Gloss polyurethane varnish

1 For the mold, cut a piece of cardboard 14 x 2½ in. Divide into four sections, each 3½ in. long; score between each with a blunt knife. Roll out dough to a thickness of about ⅜ in. Using the cardboard strip as a template, cut out a dough strip.

2. Bend the cardboard into a box shape (don't worry about the base; you will make this at a later stage). Join the ends of the box with adhesive tape. Cover the cardboard completely with foil.

3 Working on the baking sheet, carefully press the dough onto the box, taking care not to distort its shape. Join the ends and seal them with dough paste. Smooth the surface of the dough with a damp (not wet) pastry brush.

4 Now model the shells by hand. Once you have made a selection of shells, arrange them on the box. Attach with dough paste.

5 Bake the box until it is hard enough to handle. Remove the foil mold, leaving box on sheet. Immediately roll another piece of dough to a thickness of about ⅜ in. Transfer the dough to the baking sheet and carefully place the shell box on top of it. Cut around the shell box so that the raw dough underneath becomes its base. (The warmth from the shell box should seal it to the base.) Put the box back in the oven to finish baking.

6 When the box is baked inside and out, remove from the oven and let it cool. To paint, apply a thin wash of orange paint all over the box and shells. Highlight certain areas of the shells by dabbing on and rubbing in a tiny amount of black paint. Finally, varnish.

Style File

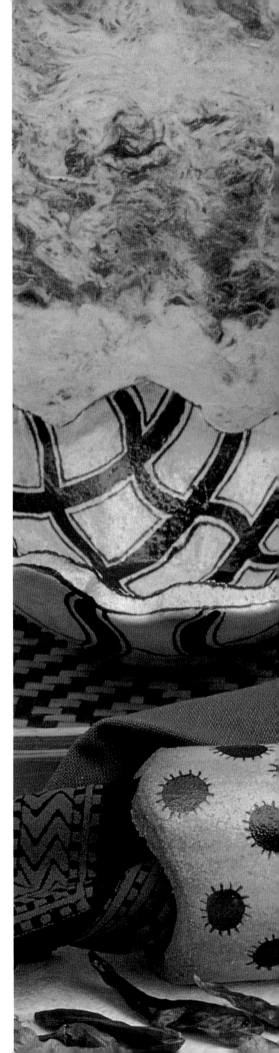

A nation's character and style are reflected in its craft work.
Some designs are handed down through generations of
model-makers, potters, or needleworkers, while others are
simply modern interpretations of traditional themes.
Each project in this section uses salt dough to echo
the characteristics of traditional crafts. The merest hint of
ethnic patterning or color is often all it takes to convey the
flavor of a design, so historical accuracy isn't important.
Vary shapes and paint finishes as much as you like. But do
try to keep surface decorations simple, for the most
effective results possible.

HOME-SWEET-HOME PLAQUE

Welcoming a friend or relative to their new home with a handmade gift is a charming tradition. If you model this project with someone special in mind, the result couldn't be more personal. Simply cut out the plaque, attach the frame, and then adapt the picture inside to suit the occasion. For example, you may prefer daisies to tulips —or why not model the house to look like the one your friend has moved into? Layers of relief work make this plaque quite thick, so tap test your dough during baking to judge the cooking time.

Before beginning, please read "Materials and Techniques," pp. 10–21. Work directly on the baking sheet.

MATERIALS AND EQUIPMENT

Salt dough (see page 12)
Dough paste (see page 13)
Nonstick baking sheet
Ruler
Rolling pin
House and tulip templates (page 133)
Small kitchen knife
Small wooden spatula
Pastry brush
Spatula
18-gauge wire, about 2¼ in.
Wire cutters
Round-ended pliers
Paintbrushes for applying dough paste,
paints, and varnish
Gold and other desired colors of
water-based paints
Gloss polyurethane varnish

1 Roll out dough to a thickness of about ¼ in. Cut out a rectangle of dough about 6¾ x 6 in. Make a frame by rolling four dough sausages ⅜ in. thick (two 6¾ in. long, two 6 in. long). Attach them to the base shape with dough paste.

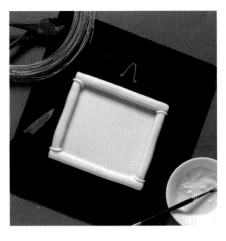

2 Roll thin sausages of dough and attach them over the corners of the dough frame. These will disguise the joints in the frame. Score in the line detail on the frame. With the wire, make a hanging loop. Embed this in the top of the plaque.

3 Roll out more dough to a thickness of about ¼ in. Cut around the house template. Attach this shape at center, about 3¼ in. above the frame. Now cut out a door and 2 windows and attach to the house with dough paste. Score the window detail. Roll a small ball of dough for the doorknob and attach. Cut out fine strips of dough with the sharp knife and attach these vertically to the roof. Score fine, horizontal lines.

4 Cut around the templates to make five tulips from the rolled-out dough. Attach the tulips, about ⅝ in. above the inner edge of the frame. Make stalks by cutting out short, narrow strips of dough; attach with dough paste. Now model small leaves, score veins, and attach a leaf next to each tulip stem with dough paste. For the buds, roll small balls of dough, attach them between the tulips, and make an indentation in each.

5 Add two leaves and a bud to the top left- and right-hand corners of the picture. Bake the plaque, tap testing it to be sure it is hard, remove from the oven, and let it cool. Paint the plaque using the finished photograph as a guide. Highlight the frame with a little gold paint, brushed on with quick strokes and a dry paintbrush. When dry, varnish.

PATCHWORK FRAME

This frame is simple to make and easy to adapt to suit your own ideas. The front surface has been scored to produce a patchwork effect, and flexible wire loops have been embedded in the back of the frame to hold photographs or pictures in place.

A handmade finish gives home-produced patchwork its special appeal, so slight imperfections will add to this project's charm. If you prefer patterned patches, before varnishing, paint your own designs in all of the squares, or paint patterned and plain patches. The finished frame should be simple and eye-catching—so stick to a few, carefully-chosen colors for a truly traditional effect.

Before beginning, please read "Materials and Techniques," pp. 10–21.

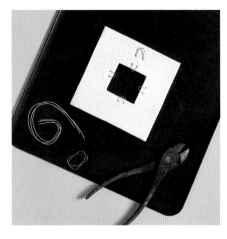

1 Working directly on baking sheet, roll out dough to a thickness of about ³⁄₈ in. Lay the frame template on top of the dough and cut around it with the knife. Tidy any rough edges with the spatula or damp pastry brush.

2 Cut four pieces of 24-gauge wire about 1¼ in. long. Treat each piece of wire as though you were making a hanging loop. Now embed the hooks in the back of the frame, position them according to the photograph. Make a hanging loop from the 2³⁄₄ in. length of 18-gauge wire. Embed it in the frame.

MATERIALS AND EQUIPMENT

Salt dough (see page 12)
Dough paste (see page 12)
Nonstick baking sheet
Ruler
Rolling pin
Frame template (page 134)
Small kitchen knife
Small wooden spatula
Pastry brush
Paintbrushes for applying dough paste,
paints, and varnish
18-gauge wire, about 2³⁄₄ in.
24-gauge wire, about 4¼ in.
Wire cutters
Round-ended pliers
Water-based paints
Gloss polyurethane varnish

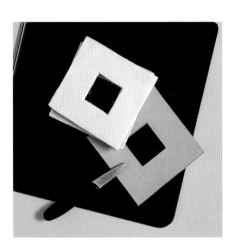

3 Half-bake the frame face down. Meanwhile, roll out more dough, this time to a thickness of about ¼ in. Following step 1, cut out another frame. When the first frame is half-baked, take it from the oven and carefully turn it over. Lay the raw dough on top of the half-baked frame. (The warmth from the lower frame should seal both pieces together.)

4 Seal all edges with dough paste, filling and smoothing any gaps as you go. Using the sharp knife, score in the patchwork squares and stitching detail. Return the frame to the oven and bake through. Paint, using the finished photograph as a guide. Varnish.

FOLK CANDLESTICKS

This project relies on simplicity for impact. Inspired by European folk art, these hanging candlesticks put traditional design to practical use.

Just roll and coil three dough sausages by hand. Connect and flatten the shapes, then strengthen them with wire loops. You can make the surface design unique by painting it to suit your own taste and decor. If you decide to use your own color scheme, bear in mind that bright patterns tend to contrast better with darker base shades. Choose a few vivid colors for your pattern work and use a fine-bristle brush to produce a delicate finish.

Because of the flammability of the varnish finish, use these candlesticks with an unlit votive candle for decoration only.

Before beginning, please read "Materials and Techniques," pp. 10–21.

MATERIALS AND EQUIPMENT

Salt dough (see page 12)
Dough paste (see page 13)
Nonstick baking sheet
Ruler
Rolling pin
Candleholder template (page 134)
Small kitchen knife
Small wooden spatula
Pastry brush
Paintbrushes for applying dough paste,
paints, and varnish
18-gauge wire, about 15 in.
Wire cutters
Round-ended pliers
Aluminum foil
Votive candle
Water-based paints
Gloss polyurethane varnish

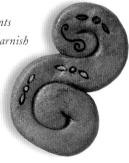

1 Working directly on the baking sheet, by hand, roll a sausage of dough about 11 in. long and about ¾ in. thick. Roll two more sausages this time about 10¼ in. long and about ¾ in. thick.

2 Bend the middle of the longest dough sausage into an inverted U shape. Roll the remaining tail pieces into coils. Bend the other two sausages into neatly coiled S shapes.

3 To join these three dough shapes together as shown in the photograph, press gently and seal with dough paste. With a rolling pin, roll over all the shapes lightly, applying even pressure as you roll. Smooth the surface with the pastry brush.

4 Cut four pieces of wire, about 1¼ in. long. Bend each piece as though you were making a hanging loop. Push the ends of the wire into the dough above and below each side joining (see photograph). About ½ in. of each loop should remain outside the dough. Make a hanging loop from 2¾ in. of wire; embed it into the dough.

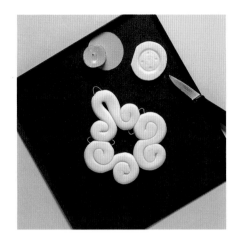

5 Working directly on the baking sheet, roll out dough to a thickness of about ³⁄₈ in. Cut around the candleholder stand template. Smooth and tidy any rough edges with the spatula. Press the votive candle into the dough to make a small, raised lip around the base. (The indentation left by the votive candle will eventually hold it in place.)

6 To decorate the candleholder, score a line around the raised lip with the point of the knife. Now score zigzags around the inner edge. Cut two 3½ in. lengths of wire and bend the ends into small loops. Keeping the candleholder flat on the baking sheet, embed both wires about 1¼ in. apart into the top of the dough.

7 To prepare the candleholder for baking, scrunch up some foil to make a support for the two wires—this will keep them from drooping in the oven. Bake the candlestick, remove from the oven, and allow to cool.

8 Paint the candlestick, using the photographs as a guide, and then varnish. Attach the candleholder stand to the base shape by pushing the wires through two inner loops of the base shape. Now bend the wires behind the base shape and fold them forward, to hook decoratively over the front of the candlestick.

MEXICAN WALL BOWL

Washes of warm color give this wall bowl a slightly faded, sun-soaked quality. To achieve this effect brush diluted paint over the base of the plaque in long, stroking movements, and then apply contrasting colors between the scored lines on the bowl. Unvarnished dough is extremely porous, so try not to overload your paintbrush (too much diluted paint will seep down through the surface, soaking your doughcraft).

The bowl itself is molded over a "pocket" of aluminum foil and you may find this technique useful for making other containers of different sizes. Just reduce or enlarge the dimensions to make smaller or larger bowls and either copy the decorative ideas used here, or reproduce colors and patterns from any number of traditional sources.

Before beginning, please read "Materials and Techniques," pp. 10–21.

MATERIALS AND EQUIPMENT

Salt dough (see page 12)
Dough paste (see page 13)
Nonstick baking sheet
Ruler
Rolling pin
Template (page 134, optional)
Aluminum foil
Small kitchen knife
Small wooden spatula
Pastry brush
*Paintbrushes for applying dough paste,
paints, and varnish*
Water-based paints
Gloss polyurethane varnish

1 Make a mold for the bowl by shaping foil into a hollow, half-circle "pocket" about 4¾ in. across and about 1 in. high. The foil must be sturdy, so make it about ⅜ in. thick.

2 Roll out dough to thickness of ⅜ in. Cut out a rectangle, about 5 x 6¼ in. or use the template. Tidy any rough edges with the spatula and smooth the surface with a damp pastry brush. Using the end of a paintbrush, make a hanging hole at the top of the rectangle.

3 Roll out more dough to a thickness of ⅜ in., carefully lay the dough over the foil "pocket" mold, and trim away any excess.

4 With the knife, cut away the top of the bowl in a continuous, wavy line. Now add a surface pattern by scoring the dough with the point of the knife.

5 Bake the dough-covered mold and the rectangular piece of dough side by side on the same baking sheet. When the dough is half-baked (hard to the touch and solid enough to handle without distortion), carefully remove the foil mold from the bowl.

6 Taking advantage of the fact that both dough pieces are still warm, join them together. The heat from the bowl and rectangle should seal them together. Join any gaps between the pieces with thickened dough paste. Return to the oven to finish baking. When cool, paint your wall bowl. When the paint has dried, varnish.

ETHNIC BOWL AND NAPKIN RINGS

Make the most of the natural tones of baked dough by displaying the napkin rings and bowl (pictured opposite) on a wooden table or shelf, or against a stark, contrasting background. These projects have been baked to varying shades of brown and then decorated with a bold, but simple, design. Both have fluted edges, created quite simply by cutting a wavy line into the raw dough. The ethnic bowl was molded over a 6 in. ovenproof bowl. If you would rather make a larger version, for fruit or potpourri, use a bigger ovenproof bowl. The same instructions apply, no matter how large or small a bowl you choose.

The napkin rings are molded over cardboard tubes. Be sure to cover each tube completely, inside and out, with foil. As long as you roll your dough out to an even thickness, join all seams securely, and smooth any rough edges while the dough is still soft enough to handle, the end result should be neat, strong, and very professional. Although the napkin rings are painted to match the bowl, you may prefer a more personal finish. Either use other paint effects from this book, or how about reproducing the design on your favorite piece of crockery or table linen? If you are not confident enough to commit yourself to a more elaborate pattern, bake a plain tile of dough along with your napkin rings and use it as a practice piece.

Before beginning, please read "Materials and Techniques," pp. 10–21.

TO MAKE THE ETHNIC NAPKIN RING

MATERIALS AND EQUIPMENT

Salt dough (see page 12)
Dough paste (see page 13)
Nonstick baking sheet
Ruler
Rolling pin
Cardboard tube (to make the napkin ring,
about 1½ in. in diameter)
Ovenproof bowl (to make the ethnic bowl,
about 6 in. in diameter)
Aluminum foil
Small kitchen knife
Small wooden spatula
Pastry brush
Paintbrushes for applying dough paste,
paints, and varnish
Black water-based paint
Gloss polyurethane varnish

1 For each ring, cut the cardboard tube to a length of about 4 in. Cover the tube, both inside and out, with foil. Smooth the foil-covered surface until absolutely flat.

2 Roll out the dough to a thickness of about ⅜ in. Cut out a strip of dough about 2 x 7½ in. Now cut a wavy line along each side of the dough strip. Smooth the surface and tidy any rough edges.

3 Carefully wrap the dough strip around the middle of the foil mold. Leave about 1 in. of the mold jutting out at each end. Join the two ends of the dough strip, cutting off excess dough and smoothing any rough edges. Make sure that the joining is well-sealed with dough paste and smoothed off neatly.

4 Stand the mold and ring upright on the baking sheet. Half-bake the dough ring until it is hard to the touch (tap to test), and strong enough to handle without distorting its shape.

5 Remove the tube mold and return to the oven to finish baking. When the dough ring is fully baked, turn the oven to a higher setting and brown in an upright position. Allow it to cool. Paint as for the ethnic bowl, opposite, and varnish.

TO MAKE THE ETHNIC BOWL

1 Cover an ovenproof bowl with foil, taking care to smooth the surface and to tuck the ends over the edge of the bowl— about 2 in. of the foil should overlap inside the bowl. Roll out the dough to an even thickness of about ³⁄₈ in. Carefully place the dough over the foil-covered bowl. Trim off any excess around the edges with the knife, taking care not to cut into the foil.

2 Smooth the surface with a damp pastry brush. Cut a wavy line around the rim with the knife. Take care not to cut into the foil. Smooth any rough edges with a damp paintbrush and/or a spatula.

3 Half-bake the bowl, remove the foil-covered mold, and return to the oven, right side up, to finish baking. When the bowl is baked through, turn the oven temperature up and let it brown.

4 When the bowl has baked to a rich brown, take it from the oven and allow to cool. Paint the pattern with black water-based paint, using the photograph as a guide. When dry, varnish.

MOLDED HEART

This molded heart has the same "sun-baked" finish as the ethnic bowl and napkin rings (see pages 66–7).

The flexibility of salt dough makes it ideal for molding over foil. But, when using handmade foil molds, resist any temptation to smooth and flatten your raw dough to perfection. The dappled gold color produced by baking actually enhances slight surface flaws, and it would be a shame to lose this effect. Browning in the oven isn't difficult, but keep an eye on your project. If the heart isn't baked enough, it will look pale and lifeless—too much, and it will become brittle and burnt. A boldly-painted pattern contrasts beautifully with this natural background.

Before beginning, please read "Materials and Techniques," pp. 10–21.

1 Working directly on the baking sheet, roll out the dough to about ³⁄₈ in thick. Lay the cardboard heart template on top of the dough and cut around the shape carefully.

2 Roll foil between your palms to make a ball. Flatten one side of the foil to make a dome shape. This should measure about 4 in. across the base and be about 1¹⁄₄ in. high.

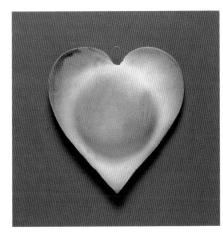

3 Place the foil dome on the baking sheet. Lift the dough heart and position it carefully over the dome. Pat and smooth the outer rim of the dough heart until it lies flat on the baking sheet, and tidy any rough edges with the spatula. Smooth the surface of the dough heart with a damp (not wet) pastry brush.

4 Make a hanging loop from the wire and embed the looped ends in the top of the heart, leaving about 2 in. protruding outside the dough. Half-bake the heart until it is hard enough to handle without distorting. Remove the foil mold, and return to the oven to finish baking. Then turn the oven to a higher setting and brown. When cool, paint as for the ethnic bowl on page 67, and then varnish.

AFRICAN DOLLS

Threaded like puppets, and designed to slip and move on their wires, these African dolls almost come to life in your hands.

Although measurements are included in the instructions, they are just a rough guide to help you judge the doll's proportions. Don't worry if your dough shapes differ slightly from these measurements in length and width, but do try to keep their thicknesses a consistent 1 in., so that they all take the same amount of time to bake. You should bake the body sections to as natural-looking a finish as possible. Wait until each section blushes from pale tan to golden brown, then allow the dough to deepen to the shades you find most pleasing. The final moments of the browning process are the most critical. When you are happy with the color of your dough, take the body sections out of the oven immediately (if you hesitate, the dough could burn). Let each piece cool completely before painting. When you varnish the dough shapes, use a small brush and take care not to clog the threading holes. Each coat of varnish should be allowed to dry thoroughly before the next is applied. The step-by-step instructions explain how to make the female doll. To make the male version (shown here and on page 75), follow steps 1 to 4 (leaving out obvious, anatomical differences) and then see the italic instructions on page 73. Don't thread the doll too tightly—your dough pieces should slip slightly on the wires to allow for movement.

Before beginning, please read "Materials and Techniques," pp. 10–21.

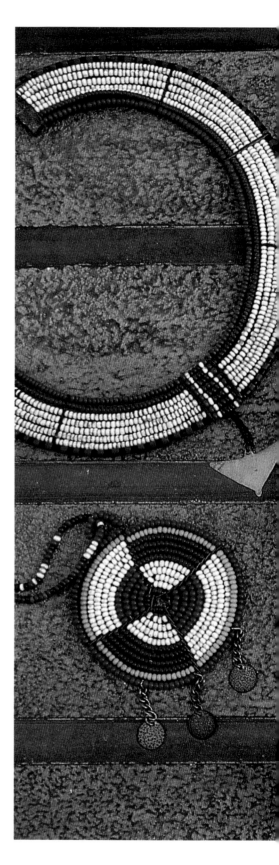

TO MAKE THE FEMALE DOLL

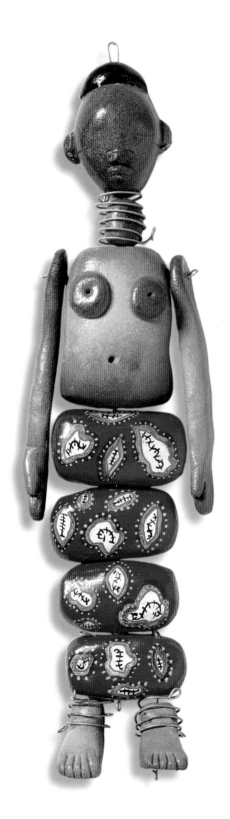

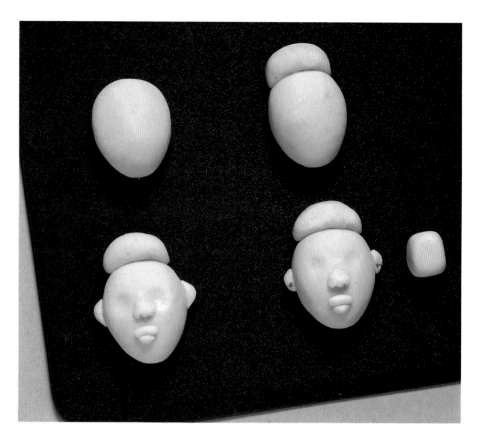

MATERIALS AND EQUIPMENT

Salt dough (see page 12)
Dough paste (see page 13)
Nonstick baking sheet
Ruler
Rolling pin
Small kitchen knife
Small wooden spatula
Pastry brush
Paintbrushes for applying dough paste,
paints, and varnish
18-gauge wire, about 2 yd. 6 in.
Wire cutters
Round-ended pliers
Red, black, yellow, and white
water-based paints
Gloss polyurethane varnish

1 To make the doll's head, roll an oval-shaped ball of dough by hand, about 1½ in. long and 1⅜ in. across. To make the hair, roll a smaller oval-shaped ball and attach it to the head with a little dough paste. Attach a small roll of dough to each side of the head, and mold into ears. Add eye sockets by pressing lightly into the dough with your finger. For the mouth make two small sausage shapes and attach with dough paste. Roll a small, triangular piece of dough for the nose. Attach and then pierce two small holes (for nostrils) with the point of the knife. Cut two 1 in. lengths of wire and push through ears (these will stay in during and after baking). The neck is a tube-shaped roll of dough, about 1 in. long and ⅝ in. wide. Flatten the back of the head and neck by pressing them gently onto the baking sheet.

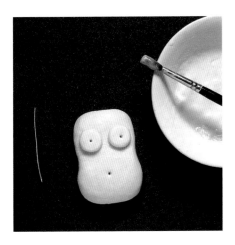

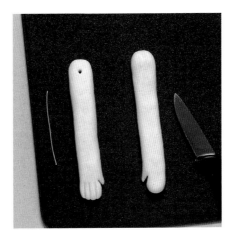

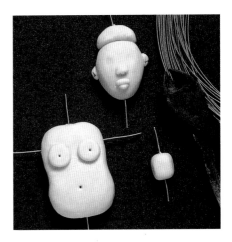

2 For the doll's torso, roll a thick sausage of dough. Pat gently into a squarer shape, about 2¾ x 2 in., keeping the surface and edges natural-looking and the back flat. Squeeze the dough to shape a waist. Flatten two balls of dough for breasts and attach with dough paste. Indent each one with the end of some wire and make a third indentation in the stomach.

3 To make the arms, roll two sausages about 4¾ in. long. Flatten the undersides. Squash the end of each arm into a paddle shape. Score lines with the knife to make fingers and thumbs. Trim the end of each thumb to make it shorter than the fingers. Make holes at the top of the arms with a piece of wire (make sure that they don't close up when baking).

4 Taking care not to distort the dough, guide a piece of wire through the head, neck, and torso. The wire should pass through the dough shape, with about 1 in. jutting out at each end. In the same way guide a piece of wire through the top of the torso, horizontally (this wire will stay in place after baking). The wires must not touch inside the dough shape.

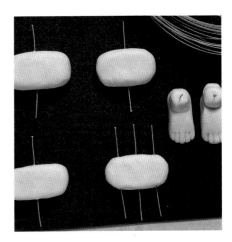

5 To make the lower half of the doll, roll a thick sausage of dough. Pat into an oblong with rounded edges—the finished piece should be about 2⅜ in. wide and 1¼ in. long. Now make three more similar, but shorter, pieces about 2 in. wide and 1¼ in. long. All dough pieces should have flat backs.

6 To make the feet, roll two short sausages of dough (about 1½ in. long). Press down on the front of each piece with your thumb and gently mold into a foot about 1 in. long. Attach two small pieces of dough for the ankles with dough paste. Make sure that the soles are flat. Score lines to mark the toes.

7 Guide a length of wire through the middle of each of the four lower-body (skirt) sections. Now pass two more pieces of wire through the bottom skirt piece (the feet will be threaded to this piece). Leave about 1 in. of wire at each end. Also, guide a piece of wire down through the center of each ankle and heel.

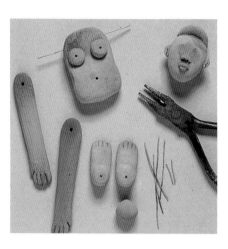

8 Bake the dough pieces in the oven. Rotate all the wires regularly to prevent the holes from closing up. Keep a close eye on the dough shapes, checking that the smaller ones don't burn. When the four lower-body sections are cooked, remove from the oven and allow to cool. Leave the other pieces in the oven to brown. Paint the four lower-body parts.

9 Check the browning process carefully. The pieces should brown unevenly (to produce natural-looking skin tones) without burning. When your dough shapes are cool, withdraw all wires except the one running across the torso. Pull the wires out very gently, using your pliers.

10 Paint the hair black and allow to dry. Varnish the painted (skirt) pieces, the head, and the remaining browned dough shapes, and leave all parts of the doll to dry.

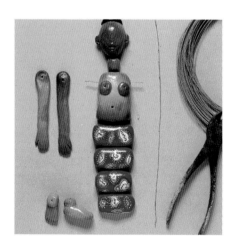

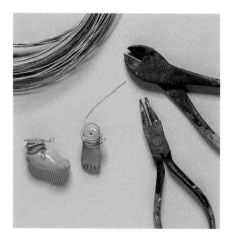

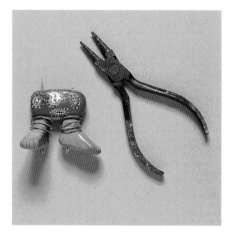

11 Calculate the length of wire needed to thread your doll by arranging the dough pieces in order. Cut enough wire to pass through the lower-body (skirt), torso, neck, and head, about $13^3/_4$ in. The wire should be long enough to pass through the dough pieces, allowing for movement, with about $^5/_8$ in. excess at each end.

12 Make ankle bracelets by cutting enough wire to wrap around each ankle four or five times—two lengths of about 10 in. Using the round-ended pliers, coil the wire around each ankle, and loop ends to neaten.

13 Thread the feet to the lower-skirt piece with two lengths of wire. Guide one piece of wire up through the left foot and through the hole in the left side of the lower-skirt piece (with ankle bracelet in place). Thread the right foot to the right side of the skirt in the same way. Make locking loops at each end of wire.

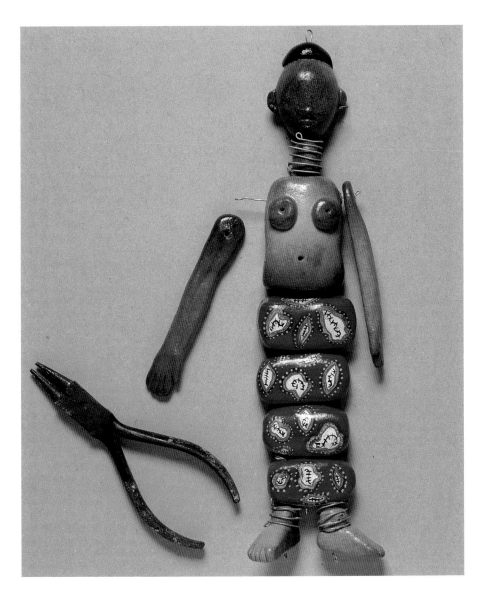

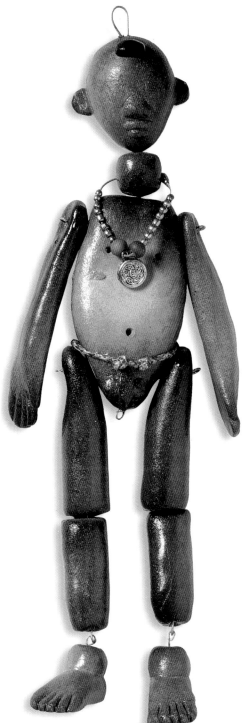

14 Make a necklace by cutting enough wire to wrap around the neck five or six times—about 13¾ in. Coil wire around the neck, and loop ends to neaten. Finish threading by guiding a wire up through the remaining hole in the lower-skirt piece, through the other three sarong pieces, torso, neck, and head. Leave room for movement between pieces, and bend a small, locking loop at each end of the wire. Attach arms by threading them onto wire ends (jutting out from upper torso). Bend locking loops to finish.

For the male doll, work steps 1–4. Wire across torso at hips (as well as at shoulders). Follow the photograph to shape leg sections and make feet as for step 6. Wire down through each leg separately. Wire feet as for female. Bake pieces. Remove wires, except at shoulder and hip. Paint and varnish pieces. Wire head and torso as for female, then attach feet to legs and legs to hips. Add a wire necklace as desired.

Feasts and Festivals

At Easter, Christmas, Thanksgiving, and Halloween —whether you're marking the occasion with a small family gathering, or throwing a bigger party for neighbors and friends—decorations with specific themes add originality and style to traditional celebrations.

The projects in this section are inspired by particular festivals. But they are just as effective in everyday surroundings —especially if you adapt them to suit your own taste and decor. Make a big impression by modeling a whole set of decorations, or choose one salt dough piece from a group of projects. Even the tiniest touch of inspiration can add something special to a room.

THE EASTER TABLE

This Easter table's centerpiece is a hen bowl that is modeled in two halves. One half is a latticework nest, while the other is molded in one piece and uses relief work and surface scoring to make the feathered head, wings, and tail.

The hen bowl is a perfect and original way of storing Easter surprises. Hand-painted (or wrapped chocolate) eggs, small gifts for children, and homemade cookies are all ideal festive treats. Or why not hide a whole family of tiny Easter chicks inside? Instructions on how to make the chicks are given on page 83.

The Easter theme continues with the simplest of napkin rings. Shaped like chicks and painted a radiant yellow, these double cleverly as egg-cup stands. Make one for each guest and arrange them around the hen centerpiece to add splashes of spring color to your Easter table.

Molded egg cups with cutaway rims create an exotic finishing touch. Paint them in rich colors, brush a swirl of gold inside each one, and your festive setting is complete.

When the festival is over, your hen bowl could be used for storing real eggs, nuts, or even small cooking implements. Although this design makes an ideal kitchen accessory, damp surroundings can damage salt dough very quickly, so keep your hen bowl away from steamy areas or places where water is in constant use.

Before beginning, please read "Materials and Techniques," pp. 10–21.

TO MAKE THE HEN LID

MATERIALS AND EQUIPMENT

Salt dough (see page 12)
Dough paste (see page 13)
Nonstick baking sheet
Ruler
Rolling pin
Wing template (page 135)
Small kitchen knife
Small wooden spatula
Ovenproof bowl (about 6 in. in diameter)
Aluminum foil
Wire for indenting detail
Pastry brush
Paintbrushes for applying dough paste, paints, and varnish
Brown, black, yellow, and red water-based paints
Gloss polyurethane varnish

1 Cover an ovenproof bowl with foil, taking care to smooth the surface. About 2 in. of the foil should overlap inside the bowl. Roll out dough to an even thickness of about ⅜ in. Place the dough over the inverted foil-covered bowl. Trim excess dough with the sharp knife. Smooth the surface with a damp pastry brush and tidy any rough edges with the spatula.

2 For the head and neck, roll a horn-shaped piece of dough about 2¾ in. long, 2 in. across, tapering to about ⅜ in. Position this shape at the "front," about 1¼ in. up from the rim. Attach with dough paste and mold into a head and neck. For the head-comb, roll three balls of dough, flatten the bases, and squeeze into wedges. Attach in a row along the front of the head.

3 The feathers are balls of dough, flattened into rounded petal shapes. Arrange the largest feathers (about ⅝ in. long, ⅜ in. wide), around the base of the neck. Overlap the feathers and make them smaller as you move toward the head. Score lines down each feather. Tease the tips of some of the feathers upward.

4 Indent eye sockets with the end of a paintbrush, attaching a ball of dough in the middle of each. Indent each ball with wire. The cheek flaps and beak are small cones of dough. Flatten their bases and attach to the face. Model the beak into a point and score a line to define the two halves. Attach a small ball of dough above the beak.

5 To make the tail, roll a thick wedge-shaped sausage of dough about 2 in. long. Attach to the back of the hen with dough paste. Disguise the joining at the base of the tail with a single layer of feathers (the same type as you used for the head and neck). They should fan out around the tail on the dough base.

6 The tail feathers are long, petal-shaped pieces of dough. Squeeze the tips into points and vary the lengths—about ⁵⁄₈ in.–1¹⁄₄ in. First, attach the shorter feathers in layers up the back of the tail with dough paste. Next, attach the longer feathers up each side and the front of the tail. Now score lines on each feather with the point of your knife.

7 Roll out dough to a thickness of about ¹⁄₄ in. Cut around template to make wings. Attach with dough paste. Using the photograph of the finished hen as a guide, score in feather patterns. Bake on the baking sheet in the oven until the dough is hard enough to handle without distorting, then take it from the oven. Carefully remove the ovenproof bowl, and peel the foil away from the inside. Return the hen lid back to the oven to finish baking.

8 When cool, brush a wash of dark brown paint over your hen. Do not paint the head-comb, eyeballs, cheek flaps, and beak. Use a small brush to dab a tiny amount of black paint onto the ends of some of the larger feathers and wings; rub in with your finger or a rag. Paint the remaining features in red and yellow. When dry, varnish.

TO MAKE THE HEN'S NEST

MATERIALS AND EQUIPMENT

Salt dough (see page 12)
Dough paste (see page 13)
Nonstick baking sheet
Ruler
Rolling pin
Small kitchen knife
Small wooden spatula
Ovenproof bowl (about 6 in. in diameter)
Aluminum foil
Pizza cutter or a long-bladed knife for
cutting strips of dough
Paintbrushes for applying dough paste,
paints, and varnish
Yellow water-based paint
Gloss polyurethane varnish

1 Cover an ovenproof bowl with foil. Roll out dough to an even thickness of ¼ in. Using the pizza cutter or long-bladed knife, cut strips of dough a little longer than the upside-down bowl and about ⅝ in. wide. Start by positioning a cross of two strips across the center of the mold. Now add more strips, weaving them over and under.

2 When the bowl is covered with woven strips, trim excess dough away from the rim. Gently squeeze the overlapping pieces at the edge so that they stick neatly together. Cut a strip of dough long enough to go around the rim of the bowl. Press gently to attach, using a little dough paste, if necessary.

3 Roll thin sausages of dough into coils and flatten them with your finger. Using the photograph as a guide, attach the decorative coils with dough paste. With the rolling pin, gently flatten the middle of your latticework since this will be the base.

4 Half-bake the nest, face down on its mold on the baking sheet. When the nest is hard enough to handle without distorting, take it from the oven. Remove the ovenproof bowl and carefully peel away the tin foil.

5 Return the nest to the oven (right side up) until it's baked through. To deepen the natural color, turn the oven to a higher setting and, keep a close eye on the dough until it browns. When cool, paint the coils yellow, let dry, and then varnish.

Templates are provided for the napkin rings and egg cups, but the chicks are modeled by hand. To make the chicks, just roll small lumps of salt dough into thick sausage shapes. Press them onto a baking sheet to make their bases firm and squeeze each dough piece into shape with your thumb and forefinger. Make small indentations for the eyes. Model tiny beaks and attach a small ball of dough above each one. After baking, paint your chicks a sunny yellow, leave their beaks a natural dough color for contrast, then varnish as usual.

TO MAKE THE CHICK NAPKIN RING

MATERIALS AND EQUIPMENT

Salt dough (see page 12)
Dough paste (see page 13)
Nonstick baking sheet
Rolling pin
Chick napkin ring template (page 135)
Small kitchen knife
Small wooden spatula
Pastry brush
Toothpick or wire
Paintbrushes for applying dough paste,
paints, and varnish
Yellow water-based paint
Gloss polyurethane varnish

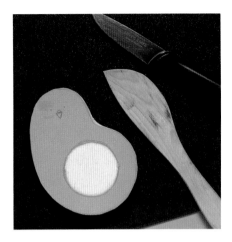

1 Roll out dough to a thickness of ³/₈ in. Place the template on top of the dough and cut around it with the kitchen knife. Smooth any rough edges with a damp paintbrush, the small spatula, or the flat side of the knife.

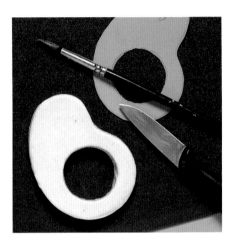

2 Cut out the circle in the middle of the template. Smooth any rough edges with a damp paintbrush.

3 Using the knife, score simple feather details on the top of the chick's head. Add eyes by pricking dough with the toothpick or wire. The beak is a tiny heart-shaped piece of dough attached to an even smaller ball of dough. Attach beak pieces with a little dough paste.

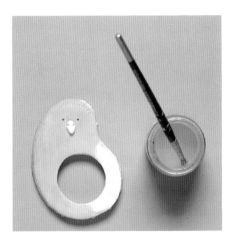

4 Bake, allow to cool. Paint the napkin ring bright yellow, leaving the chick's beak its natural dough color. Allow to dry and then varnish.

TO MAKE THE EGG CUP

MATERIALS AND EQUIPMENT

Salt dough (see page 12)
Dough paste (see page 13)
Nonstick baking sheet
Rolling pin
Egg cup template (page 135)
Small kitchen knife
Small wooden spatula
Hard-boiled egg
Ovenproof egg cup (or mold one from crumpled foil)
Aluminum foil
Pastry brush
Paintbrushes for applying dough paste, paints, and varnish
Yellow, red, and gold, water-based paints
Gloss polyurethane varnish

1 Cover a hard-boiled egg with foil, making sure that the surface is smooth. Place the foil-covered egg in an ovenproof egg cup.

2 Roll out dough to a thickness of ¼ in. Cut around circular template. Now center and place the circle of dough over the foil-covered egg. Smooth the dough over the egg with a damp pastry brush.

3 Using the photograph as a guide, cut a serrated edge into the rim of the dough, taking care not to cut into the foil. Make a flat base for your dough egg cup to stand on by flattening the top of the dough with a spatula. Half-bake the egg cup.

4 When the dough is hard enough to handle, take it out of the oven. Now lift the foil-covered egg and the dough out of the egg cup. Carefully remove the foil-covered egg and turn your dough egg cup the right way up. Return it to the oven to finish baking.

5 When baked, allow to cool—then paint, using the photograph as a guide. Allow to dry and then varnish.

CHRISTMAS DECORATIONS

No matter how exclusive they may be, shop-bought decorations can never match the originality and charm of homemade designs.

Cherubs and celestial horns make stunning tree trimmings. Paint them in bright, solid colors (deep red, burnished gold, silver, and purple contrast beautifully with the green of a Christmas tree), or use the special effects pictured here. The cherub and celestial horn were covered in washes of color and then brushed with gold to create shimmering highlights. The small holly wreath does not take long to model, so cut out and decorate as many as you can bake at one time. Paint your decorations and then apply layers of gloss varnish to make them glisten under the lights of the Christmas tree.

A large wreath loaded with fruit, berries, and nuts is the most traditional of doughcraft designs. Although the relief work is very easy to model and attach, avoid making too many shapes at one time. Cover any prepared leaves and fruits with a damp cloth (to prevent drying) until you are ready to use them. You could reduce the size of the wreath by rolling out a smaller ball of dough for the base shape. But working on too small a scale can be fussy—and it would be a shame to lose the opulence and splendor of the fully-sized version of this design.

Before beginning, please read "Materials and Techniques," pp. 10–21.

TO MAKE THE HOLLY WREATH

MATERIALS AND EQUIPMENT

Salt dough (see page 12)
Dough paste (see page 13)
Nonstick baking sheet
Rolling pin
Small kitchen knife
Small wooden spatula
Two lids (glasses or cookie cutters, one about
1¼ in. larger than the other)
Paintbrushes for applying dough paste,
paints, and varnish
Green, red, black, and gold water-based
paints
Gloss polyurethane varnish
Festive ribbon

1 Roll out dough to a thickness of ¼ in. Use the larger lid (glass or cookie cutter) to stamp out a circle in the dough. Then stamp out an inner circle with the smaller lid (glass or cookie cutter).

2 Flatten small balls of dough and shape them into leaves. Score veins. Roll tiny balls of dough to make berries.

3 Attach the leaves and berries to your dough wreath with a little dough paste.

4 Bake, and allow to cool. Paint using green for the leaves, red for the berries, and gold for highlights. When dry, varnish. Thread with festive ribbon to hang.

TO MAKE THE CHERUB

MATERIALS AND EQUIPMENT

Salt dough (see page 12)
Dough paste (see page 13)
Nonstick baking sheet
Ruler
Small kitchen knife
Small wooden spatula
18-gauge wire, about 2¼ in.
Paintbrushes for applying dough paste,
paints, and varnish
Flesh-colored and gold water-based paints
Gloss polyurethane varnish

1 Roll a sausage of dough about 2¾ in. long. Model it into a body and leg shape, about ⅜ in. thick. Roll a ball for the head and flatten it gently until the dough is about ⅜ in. thick. Attach the head to the body with dough paste.

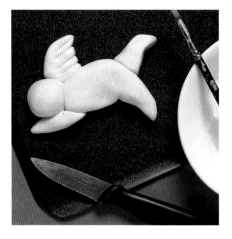

2 Flatten and shape a sausage of dough, about 1¼ in. long, into a second leg. Shape a sausage of dough 1½ in. long into an arm. Flatten a ball of dough into a petal-shaped wing. Attach the leg, arm, and wing to the cherub with dough paste. Score lines.

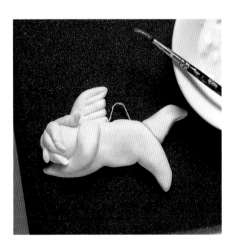

3 Roll a sausage for the second arm, about 1½ in. long, ⅜ in. thick. Attach it across the cherub with dough paste. For the hair, roll small sausages, twist each sausage, and attach to the head. Make a hanging loop from the wire. Embed it just below the wing.

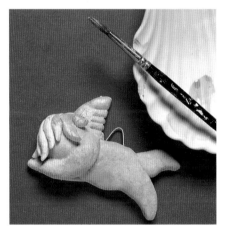

4 Bake. When the cherub is cool, apply a wash of flesh-colored paint to the body. Paint the hair and the wing gold. Lightly brush gold paint over the body to add highlights. Allow to dry and then varnish.

TO MAKE THE CELESTIAL HORN

MATERIALS AND EQUIPMENT

Salt dough (see page 12)
Dough paste (see page 13)
Nonstick baking sheet
Ruler
Small kitchen knife
Small wooden spatula
Paintbrushes for applying dough paste,
paints, and varnish
Orange and gold water-based paints
Gloss polyurethane varnish
Festive ribbon

1 Working directly on the baking sheet, roll a long sausage of dough, about 6½ in. long and ⅝ in. thick. Flatten one end of the sausage to form the horn's bell. Roll the other end into a point.

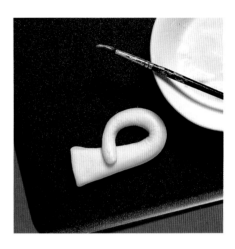

2 Curl the dough into a horn shape and secure the end with dough paste.

3 Roll three small balls and attach them with dough paste. Make a larger ball and attach it to the horn as a mouthpiece.

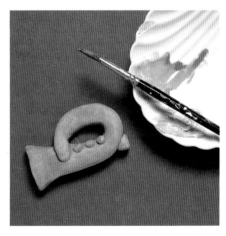

4 Bake. When cool, cover the horn with a wash of orange paint. Brush on gold paint to highlight. When the paint is dry, varnish. Thread with festive ribbon to hang.

TO MAKE THE CHRISTMAS WREATH

MATERIALS AND EQUIPMENT
Salt dough (see page 12)
Dough paste (see page 13)
Nonstick baking sheet
Rolling pin
Leaf and wreath templates (pages 131 and 135)
Small kitchen knife
Small wooden spatula
Dried cloves
Paintbrushes for applying dough paste, paints, and varnish
Rag or paper towel to apply paint finishes
Green, brown, gold, and desired fruit-colored water-based paints
Gloss polyurethane varnish

1 Working directly on the baking sheet, roll out dough to a thickness of ³/₈ in. Lay the wreath template on the dough and cut around it to make the base of the wreath. Smooth any rough edges with a damp brush or the spatula.

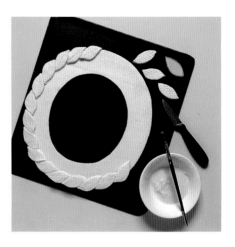

2 Roll out dough to a thickness of ¹/₄ in. Cut around the leaf template and tidy any rough edges with the spatula. Score veins. Only make as many leaves as you can attach before the dough dries out. Arrange leaves at an angle, creating an even border around the wreath's outer edge. Bend the leaves slightly, so they overlap the edges of the base shape. Attach with dough paste.

3 To make pears, roll balls of dough by hand and model them into pear shapes. Push a dried clove into the bottom of each pear, flower end out, and another into the top, stalk end out. To make plums, roll smaller balls of dough. Squeeze the ends into points. Attach with dough paste.

4 To make apples and oranges, roll balls of dough by hand. Add a dried clove stalk to the top of each dough apple. Add a dried clove flower to the top of each dough orange. Attach with dough paste.

5 To make grapes, berries, and nuts, roll small balls of dough by hand. Attach the grapes to your wreath in long bunches. Attach the berries to the wreath in groups. Indent the center of each berry with the end of a paintbrush. Attach the nuts to your wreath in groups. Use dough paste to attach the grapes, berries, and nuts.

6 To make small leaves, flatten small balls of dough and shape them into leaves. Score veins. Position three leaves above the grapes, as in the photograph. Attach these small leaves with dough paste. Use them to fill gaps in the arrangement, tucking them under the edges of fruits to make the overall effect thick and lush.

7 Bake the wreath. When it has cooled completely, paint the wreath. To make the outer leaves rich and festive, paint them green and dab on brown paint for contrast.

8 Paint the fruits with a base wash in their natural colors, dabbing on darker tones for contrast. Paint the smaller leaves bright green. When the paint is dry, use an almost-dry paintbrush (wipe excess paint off the bristles) to brush on gold paint sparingly over the outside leaves. Varnish.

WHEAT PLAQUE

Highly decorative and particularly traditional, this project is also very simple to make. The custom of fashioning wheat sheaves from bread dough is hundreds of years old, but because this dough contains salt, it will be more durable than most edible bread mixtures. Varnishing deepens the golden tones of baked dough and provides a protective seal, which should prolong the life of your plaque still further.

Take advantage of this project's simplicity by leaving the baked dough its natural color. Once you have covered the basic plaque shape with layers of wheat and a sprinkling of cornflowers, the only highlights necessary are a touch of blue for the cornflowers and a subtle brush of yellow on the ears of grain.

Before beginning, please read "Materials and Techniques," pp. 10–21.

MATERIALS AND EQUIPMENT

Salt dough (see page 12)
Dough paste (see page 13)
Nonstick baking sheet
Ruler
Rolling pin
Wheat plaque template (page 136)
Small kitchen knife
Small wooden spatula
18-gauge wire, about 2¼ in.
Wire cutters
Round-ended pliers
Garlic press
Paintbrushes for applying dough paste,
paints, and varnish
Yellow and blue water-based paints
Gloss polyurethane varnish
Rope or natural-colored raffia
for decoration

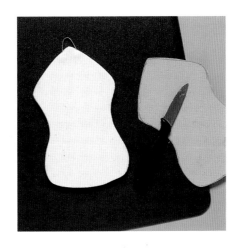

1 Working directly on the baking sheet, roll out dough to thickness of ³⁄₈ in. Cut around the wheat template. Tidy any rough edges with the spatula. Make a hanging loop from the wire. Embed the loop in the top of the dough shape.

2 Squeeze dough through the garlic press. Brush a small amount of dough paste directly onto the base and then lay each bunch of strands onto the dough base shape. Starting from the top, work your way down the base shape in layers, over-lapping the ends of the dough strands as you go.

3 To make ears of wheat, model small leaf shapes by hand. Score lines with the point of the knife. Attach the ears of wheat to the top half of the plaque with dough paste (use the photograph as a guide, or create your own arrangement).

4 To make cornflowers, roll balls of dough by hand. Attach to the plaque with dough paste. Using the end of a paint-brush, indent the center of each ball. Now make petal shapes by scoring lines around the indentation. Bake the plaque (tap to test). Turn the oven to a higher setting and brown for a natural effect.

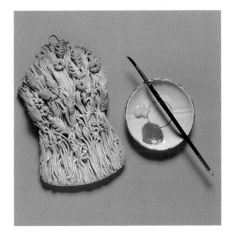

5 Leave the plaque its natural baked color, but add touches of blue by painting the cornflowers. Dip a dry brush into some yellow paint (wipe off excess) and brush lightly over the ears of wheat. Tie rope or natural-colored raffia around the middle to decorate.

HORN OF PLENTY

Whether you use it as a wall bowl or as the centerpiece for a festive table—a horn of plenty makes a beautiful and practical decoration.

This model is made up of two simple shapes—a flat, rectangular plaque and a long, curved bowl—which are joined together and trimmed to fit.

Aluminum foil is used for the mold because it is very versatile and flexible. A good mold should be strong enough to support the dough throughout baking, so scrunch the foil into a compact wad. Bend the wad into a horn shape, and then drape your dough over it. The instructions include measurements, but don't worry about small variations in size. If you use your own foil mold as a guide, the finished horn should stay in proportion, even if its dimensions differ slightly from those supplied here.

Before beginning, please read "Materials and Techniques," pp. 10–21.

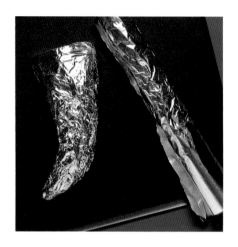

1 Working directly on the baking sheet, first make a mold for the dough. Do this by scrunching foil into a hollow, horn-shaped pocket. The mold should be about 11¾ in. long, about 8 in. wide at its widest point, and about 2⅜ in high.

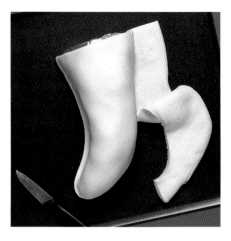

2 Roll out dough to a thickness of about ⅜ in. Drape the dough over the foil mold and gently squeeze it into shape. Trim off any excess dough and smooth any rough edges.

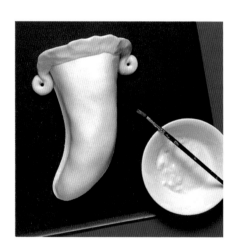

3 Roll a sausage of dough, about 2⅜ in. longer than the opening of the horn. Attach this around the opening with dough paste, leaving 1¼ in. trailing on either side. Squeeze the sausage between your thumb and forefinger to produce a wavy effect. Roll the tails of the sausage inward to form coils. Push a hole through each coil with the end of a paintbrush.

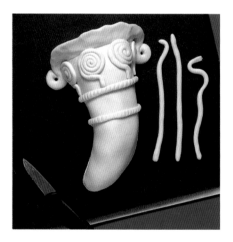

4 The top coils are simply hand-rolled sausages of dough. Coil them into spirals, leaving short, decorative tailpieces curling downward. Arrange and attach them around the top section of the horn with dough paste. Make decorative ropes by rolling thin sausages of dough by hand. Attach them at intervals across the horn and score lines to produce a rope effect.

5 Make decorative studs by rolling small balls of dough. Flatten the balls, attach them to the horn with dough paste, and then indent each one with the end of a paintbrush. Half-bake the horn until it is hard enough to handle without distorting. Carefully remove the foil mold.

6 Roll out dough to an even thickness of ³/₈ in. The dough should be wider than the horn and about 2 in. longer at the top. Press the half-baked horn onto the dough. Cut around the horn and shape the raw dough at the top into a half-circle. Re-pierce the side holes. The warmth of the horn should seal it to the dough base.

8 Put the horn back in the oven to bake through. When it's cool, paint your horn of plenty in rich, vibrant colors, using the photographs as a guide. Varnish when the paint is dry.

7 Add a trimming to the top edge of the half-circle by attaching a hand-rolled sausage of dough and scoring in a rope effect. Pierce a hanging hole through the top of the base with end of paintbrush. Now trim off excess dough and fill any gaps between the horn and its new base with thickened dough paste.

PUMPKIN PLAQUE

Although this pumpkin plaque is a perfect Halloween decoration, the various, soft greens of its leaves and the subtle orange washes of the pumpkin itself also make it a beautiful year-round ornament.

The pumpkin is simply made from lengths (or sausages) of hand-rolled dough, molded over a foil dome. The ends of the longest roll extend and coil outward to provide a base for the leaves and vine tails.

Before beginning your project, please read "Materials and Techniques", pages 10–21. Because it will eventually hang on a wall, the back of the pumpkin plaque should be as flat as possible. So, work directly on your baking sheet and gently press any smaller shapes (like the tips of overhanging leaves) onto the surface to keep their backs level. Use a damp paintbrush to smooth and blend the pumpkin sections into place.

MATERIALS AND EQUIPMENT

Salt dough (see page 12)
Dough paste (see page 13)
Nonstick baking sheet
Rolling pin
Vine leaf template (page 130)
Small kitchen knife
Small wooden spatula
Aluminum foil
18-gauge wire, about 2¼ in.
Wire cutters
Round-ended pliers
Paintbrushes for applying dough paste,
paints, and varnish
Rag or paper towel to apply paint finishes
Orange, brown, and green
water-based paints
Gloss polyurethane varnish

1 Working directly on the baking sheet, roll some aluminum foil into a ball and press it down on the baking sheet to flatten its base. You should now have a dome of foil measuring about 1¼ in. high and 3½ in. across the base.

2 Roll a long sausage of dough about 26 in. long and about ¾ in. thick. Place the foil dome against the central point of the sausage and bend the dough around the edge of the foil dome. Join together at the top of the dome, applying a little dough paste. Make sure that the "tails" of dough left over are equal in length. Now coil the tails, using the photograph as a guide.

3 Gently flatten the coiled tail pieces with the palm of your hand. Using the 2¾ in. length of wire, make a hanging loop. Embed the ends of the loop in the top of the plaque.

4 Roll six dough sausages—about 6 in. long and about ½ in. wide. Gently squeeze the ends of each sausage into a point. Now lay the dough sausages side by side over the foil mold. When the mold is covered, fill and seal any gaps with thickened dough paste. Smooth any untidy edges at the top and base of the pumpkin.

5 Mould a small sausage of dough into a stalk shape. Squeeze the end into a point; attach with dough paste. Roll out dough to a thickness of ⅜ in. Using the vine leaf template, cut out six leaves. Score veins with the point of the knife. Overlap some of the leaves, bend the ends slightly, and attach with dough paste.

6 Roll three very thin sausages. Drape them across the leaves. Secure with dough paste. Half-bake the plaque, remove the foil mold, and return to the oven to finish baking. Paint the pumpkin with thin washes of orange. Paint the leaves with washes of green; dab on brown shading while still damp. When dry, varnish.

Special Occasions

Whether you are celebrating the birth of a baby, an
anniversary, a wedding, or simply celebrating for the sake
of it, a special occasion is a perfect excuse to be creative.
Handmade gifts and decorations transform anniversaries
and celebrations into memorable occasions, especially when
they are designed with someone special in mind.
This section should encourage you to indulge your natural
sense of color and style. If you don't have the confidence to
use the projects as patterns for your own designs, add a
touch of individuality by making smaller changes in color
or surface pattern, for example.

VALENTINE
HEARTS

The heart is a charming romantic symbol and its shape is extremely rewarding to decorate. Relief work and uncomplicated paint effects can turn the simplest of salt dough shapes into something special within minutes. This group of projects shows you just how adaptable a single molded heart design can be.

Compact in size and very simple to make, the small Heart of Gold on this page is a good starting point. It uses the same basic molding technique as the larger hearts pictured opposite, but only needs a wash of color and some burnished highlights as decoration.

Like the small gold heart, the larger hearts are simply raw dough shapes, draped and trimmed over an aluminum foil dome. The instructions show you how a little flair and ingenuity can give each one a very distinctive finish.

The Coiled and Swirled Hearts are edged with hand-rolled decoration. Bright, contrasting colors are used to emphasize this relief work on the Coiled Heart, but in the case of the Swirled Heart, a rub-off paint effect produces a deep bronze sheen surrounding a pattern on the raised center. The Cutout Heart's uncluttered lines and surface scoring provide its impact. A sharp, clean zigzag design in darker paint creates an eye-catching frame for the inner cutout shape. The dramatic Cupid's Arrow Heart is pierced before baking. When the heart has been painted and varnished, a twisted wire arrow is threaded through the holes.

Before beginning, please read "Materials and Techniques," pp. 10–21.

MATERIALS AND EQUIPMENT

Salt dough (see page 12)
Dough paste (see page 13)
Nonstick baking sheet
Ruler
Rolling pin
Heart template (page 136)
Small kitchen knife
Small wooden spatula
Aluminum foil
Pastry brush
Spatula
18-gauge wire, about 2¾ in.
Wire cutters
Round-ended pliers
Paintbrushes for applying dough paste,
paints, and varnish
Rag or paper towel to apply paint finishes
Black and gold water-based paints
Gloss polyurethane varnish

1 Working directly on the baking sheet, roll out dough to an even thickness of about ⅜ in. Lay the heart template on top of the dough and cut around the shape carefully. Roll some foil between your palms to make a ball. Flatten one side of the foil to make a dome shape that measures about 2½ in. across the base and about 1 in. high.

2 Using a spatula (to avoid distorting the dough), lay the heart over the dome. Pat and smooth the outer rim of the dough heart until it lies flat. Smooth the surface with a damp pastry brush and tidy any rough edges with the wooden spatula. Make a hanging loop from the wire. Embed the loop into the top of the heart.

3 Half-bake the heart. Remove the foil mold and return to the oven to finish baking. Allow to cool. Apply an even layer of black paint; let it dry. Now dip the soft rag into a tiny amount of gold paint and dab this onto the black surface color to produce an antique-type finish. When the paint is dry, varnish.

TO MAKE THE COILED HEART

For the Coiled and Swirled Hearts, follow steps 1–2 of Heart of Gold (see page 104), making the foil dome for both of these hearts about 4 in. across the base and about 1¼ in. high.

1 Roll thin sausages of dough and wind them into coil shapes. Attach to the flat rim of the heart with dough paste. Roll tiny balls of dough and position one between each coil. Indent each ball with the end of a paintbrush.

2. Half-bake the heart. When the dough is firm enough to handle, remove the foil mold and return to the oven to finish baking. Allow it to cool and apply a wash of purple paint (but not over the decorative balls and coils).

3 Paint the coils with red paint or with another contrasting color.

4 Paint the balls with gold paint. Highlight the coils by dabbing a tiny amount of gold paint over each one. When the paint is dry, varnish.

TO MAKE THE SWIRLED HEART

MATERIALS AND EQUIPMENT

Salt dough (see page 12)
Dough paste (see page 13)
Nonstick baking sheet
Ruler
Rolling pin
Heart template (page 137)
Small kitchen knife
Small wooden spatula
Aluminum foil
Pastry brush
Spatula
18-gauge wire, about 2¼ in. for each
hanging loop
Wire cutters
Round-ended pliers
Paintbrushes for applying dough paste,
paints, and varnish
Rag or paper towel to apply paint finishes
Purple, pink, black, and gold
water-based paints
Gloss polyurethane varnish

1 Make coils and tiny balls as in step 1 opposite. Attach the coils and balls to the rim of the heart with dough paste. Gently flatten the surface of each ball. To make the detail at the lower point, roll two coils, leaving a tail of dough trailing from each. Position them as in the photograph.

2 Half-bake the heart. When the dough is firm enough to handle, remove the foil mold and return the heart to the oven to finish baking. Allow to cool. Paint a wash of pink over the heart (leaving the decorated rim of the heart unpainted).

3 Paint the coils, balls, and the rim of the heart in black. Next paint a swirl pattern over the middle of the heart. Allow to dry.

4 Dab gold paint over the coils, balls, and rim. Before the gold paint is completely dry, rub with a soft rag to expose patches of black. Highlight some of the swirls with dashes of gold paint. When the paint is dry, varnish your heart.

TO MAKE THE CUTOUT HEART

For the Cutout and Cupid's Arrow Hearts follow steps 1–2 of Heart of Gold (see page 104), making the foil dome for both of these hearts about 4 in. across the base about 1¼ in. high.

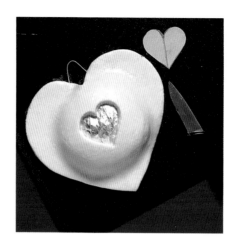

1 Cut out the inner heart with the small heart template or a cookie cutter. Apply enough pressure to cut through the dough, but avoid pressing into the foil mold. When you have made your heart-shaped cutout, smooth the inner edges. If the main heart shape has become at all distorted, gently push it back into shape.

2 Score two lines, about ¼ in. apart, around the inner heart. Make small indentations between these lines. Score two lines (about ⅛ in. apart) and about ⅜ in. in from the outer edge of the heart. Now score a zigzag pattern around the outside. Make indentations between the triangle shapes formed by the zigzags.

3 Half-bake the heart, remove the foil mold, and return to the oven to finish baking. When cool, paint the main body of the heart gold. Leave the scored lines and indentations unpainted.

4 Now paint the triangles (created by the zigzag scoring) around the outer edge. These look dramatic painted black, or choose another dark, contrasting color. When the paint is dry, varnish your heart.

TO MAKE THE CUPID'S ARROW HEART

MATERIALS AND EQUIPMENT
Salt dough (see page 12)
Dough paste (see page 13)
Nonstick baking sheet
Ruler
Rolling pin
Heart templates (page 137)
Small kitchen knife
Small wooden spatula
Small heart-shaped cookie cutter (optional)
Aluminum foil
Pastry brush
Spatula
18-gauge wire, about 2¼ in. for each hanging loop, and 20 in. for arrow
Toothpick or small piece of wire for pricking indentations
Wire cutters
Round-ended pliers
Paintbrushes for applying dough paste, paints, and varnish
Rag or paper towel to apply paint finishes
Red, gold and black water-based paints
Gloss polyurethane varnish

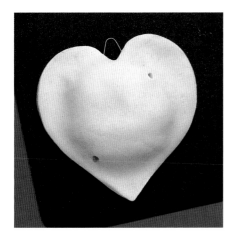

1 Make the holes for your wire arrow. Do this by pushing the end of a paintbrush through the raised part of the dough. Make one hole at a time—the first in the top right-hand side of the heart and the second in the lower left-hand side. Pierce the dough sideways, pushing your paintbrush through the dough at an angle.

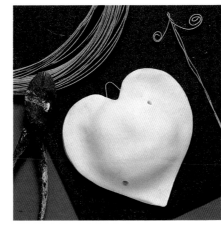

2 Half-bake the heart, remove the foil mold, and return to the oven to finish baking. To make the arrow, cut about 20 in. of wire. Fold it in half and twist loosely once or twice. Using round-ended pliers, separate the wires about 4 in. from the ends. Bend and coil each end to form the arrow tip as shown.

3 When the dough heart is baked, take it from the oven and let it cool. Give the heart a solid base coat of red paint.

4 Dab on a mottled highlight effect with a rag dipped in gold paint. When the paint is dry, varnish the heart. Allow the varnish to dry thoroughly. Finally, thread the shaft of the wire arrow through the heart.

ROLLED HEART WITH ROSES

This heart involves no templates or patterns—the whole project is modeled by hand, which makes it very easy to vary its size and thickness. The heart itself is simply a hand-rolled "sausage" which is curved into shape and then secured with dough paste. To make a smaller heart, just roll a shorter, slimmer sausage, or roll a longer, thicker piece to make a larger version of the same design.

Two hand-modeled roses are a pretty addition, but if you prefer a more elaborate finish, you could cover the whole surface with leaves and flowers. Finally, thread your heart with beads and a bell. (Add a larger hanging loop, longer wire, and more beads to a larger heart.)

Before beginning, please read "Materials and Techniques," pp. 10–21.

MATERIALS AND EQUIPMENT

Salt dough (see page 12)
Dough paste (see page 13)
Nonstick baking sheet
Ruler
Rolling pin
Small kitchen knife
Small wooden spatula
Pastry brush
18-gauge wire, about 5 in.
Wire cutters
Round-ended pliers
Paintbrushes for applying dough paste,
paints, and varnish
Water-based paints
Beads and bell
Gloss polyurethane varnish

1 Roll a dough sausage, about 10 in. long and ³/₄ in. thick, and curve it into a heart shape. Make a hanging loop with about 2³/₄ in. of wire; embed it into the heart. Cut a piece of wire, about 2³/₈ in., and bend a loop at one end. Push the loop into through the heart leaving about 1¹/₄ in. hanging down.

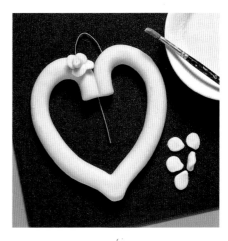

2 To make the roses, flatten a small ball of dough between your thumb and forefinger. Roll this petal into an upside-down cone shape that will form the center of the rose. Make four more petals and attach them to the bottom of the coneshape with a little dough paste. Attach a rose to each side of the heart with dough paste.

3 To make leaves, roll out dough to a thickness of about ¹/₈ in. Cut out four leaf shapes. Neaten any rough edges. Score a line down the middle of each leaf and score vein lines on each side of the central line. Attach with dough paste. (Leaves in each pair should overlap slightly.)

4 Add decoration to the heart shape by scoring two lines (about ¹/₄ in. apart) along the surface. Using the end of a paintbrush or the point of the knife, make a row of indentations inside the lines. Bake the heart.

5 When cool, paint using the photograph as a guide. Allow to dry and then varnish. Thread the beads and the bell onto the wire in the middle. Finally, bend a loop into the end of the wire to lock the threaded decorations in place.

1 Roll out dough to a thickness of about ³/₈ in. Working directly on the baking sheet, cut around the base template and the small heart shape with a sharp knife. Smooth and neaten any rough edges with the wooden spatula or damp paintbrush.

DOVE PLAQUE

This dove plaque is a very symbolic way to mark an engagement or anniversary. If you paint in the names of the couple involved, the plaque becomes even more personal—or add the date to make a lasting record of the happy event.

Templates are provided to help you cut the dough shapes. Laying dough pieces on a flat base is a very effective

way of bringing a design to life, but only if the relief work is an even thickness. For a neat finish, roll your dough out carefully, and smooth any rough edges before laying relief shapes on the base. Try not to distort the dough, and make sure that scored lines and indentations are evenly applied.

Before beginning, please read "Materials and Techniques," pp. 10–21.

2 Using the point of the knife and the ruler, score three lines, about ¹/₈ in. apart, across the plaque below the heart. Score a single line about ⁵/₈ in. above the bottom edge of the plaque, curving the line as you go, and two short vertical lines in the middle. With the 2³/₄ in. of wire, make a hanging loop. Embed the loop in the top of the plaque.

MATERIALS AND EQUIPMENT
Salt dough (see page 12)
Dough paste (see page 13)
Nonstick baking sheet
Ruler
Rolling pin
Templates (page 139)
Small kitchen knife
Small wooden spatula
Pastry brush
Spatula
18-gauge wire, about 2¼ in.
Wire cutters
Round-ended pliers
Paintbrushes for applying dough paste,
paints, and varnish
Rag or paper towel to apply paint finish
Red, pink, white, and black
water-based paints
Gloss polyurethane varnish

3 Roll out more dough, this time to a thickness of about ¼ in. Cut around the two dove templates. Smooth and tidy any rough edges.

4 Carefully lift the larger dove shape and place it on the dough plaque. Attach with dough paste. Make sure that the bottom edge of the dove shape is in line with (and touches) the curved scored line. The dove's wings should jut out beyond the edges of the plaque.

  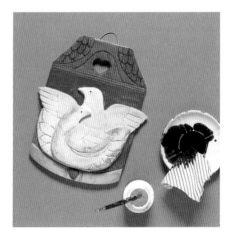

5 Lay the second dove shape on top of the first and attach with dough paste. Smooth and tidy any rough edges with the wooden spatula. With the end of a small paintbrush or the point of the knife, make an eye indentation in both dove shapes. Follow the photograph to score in the feathers and wings.

6 Cut out a tiny heart and place at the bottom of the plaque. Now score in the roof detail. The tiles on each side of the roof shape must be clearly defined, so score slightly thicker lines (by using a wider knifepoint, or by going over the same line twice). Take care not to cut too deeply. Bake your plaque, then turn the oven to a higher setting and brown.

7 When cool, paint the plaque. Use bright colors for the background, tiny heart, and roof (don't paint the space below the dove shapes). Paint the doves white or cream. When the paint is almost dry, highlight the wingtips, the necks, and the ends of the feathers by dabbing on a tiny amount of black paint with a soft rag or the tip of your forefinger. Varnish.

WEDDING PLAQUE

Decorative plaques with a personal theme make wonderful gifts—especially when they are given to commemorate a once-in-a-lifetime occasion. This wedding plaque is very easy to assemble. Small details and decorative paint effects give this plaque a special appeal. Small balls of dough squeezed through a garlic press are used to trim the bride's dress and veil, and a wash of gold over a white paint base adds a luxurious, shimmering finish to her wedding outfit.

Before beginning, please read "Materials and Techniques," pp. 10–21.

MATERIALS AND EQUIPMENT

Salt dough (see page 12)

Dough paste (see page 13)

Nonstick baking sheet

Ruler

Rolling pin

Templates (see page 138)

Small kitchen knife

Small wooden spatula

Garlic press

Pastry brush

Spatula

18-gauge wire, about 2¼ in.

Wire cutters

Round-ended pliers

Paintbrushes for applying dough paste,
paints, and varnish

Rag or paper towel to apply paint finish

White, flesh, black, gray, and gold
water-based paints

Gloss polyurethane varnish

1 Working directly on the baking sheet, roll out dough to an even thickness of ¹/₄ in. Put your template on the dough and cut around it to make the base shape of the plaque. Smooth all rough edges and correct any distortion in shape. Make a heart-shaped hanging loop from the 2³/₄ in. length of wire and embed it in the top of the plaque.

2 Roll out more dough to a thickness of ¹/₈ in. Cut around templates to make the bride's veil, the groom's jacket, and the bride and groom's faces. The dough is very thin, so use a spatula to transfer the shapes to the base shape. Position the shapes (faces first) according to the photograph and attach with dough paste. Make sure that all edges are smooth (fill any gaps with thickened dough paste).

3 Roll two sausages, each about 2 in. long and about ³/₈ in. wide. Squeeze the ends into points. Using the photograph as a guide, position the arms and attach with dough paste. Blend the edges of the arms into the base shape. Score a dividing line between the bride and groom's faces and lower bodies. Score more lines: along the bride's ankle, the groom's ankle, and one across both the bride and groom's ankles.

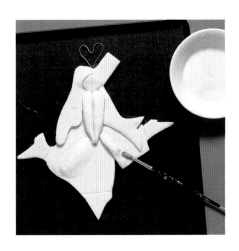

4 To create slight relief, roll two dough sausages. Place one dough sausage on the skirt and one on the trousers and blend these shapes into the base shape.

5 Roll another sausage to make the brim of the groom's hat. Roll two small dough balls, attach them to the bride and groom's faces, and shape them into noses. The groom's moustache is two small sausages of dough with pointed ends. Score the shoe laces, heels, and trouser stripes.

6 Roll a sausage of dough for the groom's cuff. Make the trim for the bride's dress and veil by squeezing dough through a garlic press. Drape some strands on the cuff and along edges of the veil and dress, attach with dough paste. Bake. Paint, using the photograph as a guide.

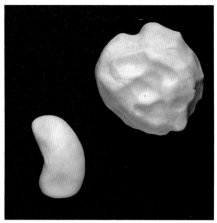

1 Working directly on the baking sheet, roll a fat sausage of dough about 2¾ in. long and about 1 in. thick. Using the photograph as a guide, model the sausage into a body shape. Make sure that the back of the dough is flat.

PAPERWEIGHTS

These paperweights are designed to make the most of the rich golden-brown of baked dough. Touches of black and/or white add contrast to hats (or hair), and the vivid scarlet of a clutched heart can be glimpsed inside each figure's grasp. Modeled by hand, the rounded contours and smooth surfaces are produced by blending the raw dough into a series of neat curves. The instructions show how to make the figure with the pointed hat. For the other two, follow the instructions, but model a wide-brimmed hat with a wavy brim for one, and make hair from small rolls of dough for the other.

Before beginning, please read "Materials and Techniques," pp. 10–21.

MATERIALS AND EQUIPMENT

Salt dough (see page 12)
Dough paste (see page 13)
Nonstick baking sheet
Ruler
Small kitchen knife
Small wooden spatula
Paintbrushes for applying dough paste,
paints, and varnish
Red, black, and white water–based paints
Gloss polyurethane varnish

2 Roll a ball of dough for the head about ³/₄ in. long and about ³/₄ in. thick. Attach the head to the body by applying dough paste and pressing gently into position. Make the heart by rolling a ball of dough, flattening the back, and indenting the top with the blunt edge of the knife. Attach the heart with dough paste and press gently into position.

3 To make the thigh, roll a thick sausage of dough about 2³/₄ in. long and about 2³/₄ in. thick. Make the top of the thigh rounder and thicker than the lower part. Attach with dough paste. Roll a sausage of dough about 3 in. long and ³/₄ in. thick, shape into a leg and foot, and attach with dough paste. Make sure that the back of the dough is flat.

4 Roll a slightly thinner sausage of dough for the arm, long enough to fit across the body and heart. Position this piece and attach it with a little dough paste. The hat is simply a ball of dough, flattened at the base and pulled into a point at the top. Mold the hat into position on top of the head (using a little dough paste to attach it). The back of the hat should be flat. Score lines across the dough with the blade of the knife.

5 Attach a tiny ball of dough for the ear. Then attach a small ball of dough for the nose, carefully blending it into shape. The eye sockets are shallow indentations, made with the end of a paintbrush. Bake the dough figure, then turn the oven to a higher setting and let it brown. When cool, paint in the stripes and spots on the hat, and paint the heart red. Wait for the paint to dry thoroughly before varnishing.

PARTY PIECES

Fantasy animals make perfect favors for children's parties. Quick and easy to produce, the technique couldn't be simpler. Just cut their shapes, using the templates provided, and use your imagination to transform the cutouts into entirely original salt dough gifts for each of your guests. When it comes to paint finishes, anything goes—either ignore realism entirely and choose bright colors and crazy patterns for maximum impact, or opt for something more subtle.

Either leave the shapes as they are or (after painting and varnishing) make them into pins by gluing pinbacks to them. These projects are designed to be adapted, so you don't have to use our templates. Make freehand shapes by cutting straight into the dough with a sharp knife, or use cookie cutters to stamp out alternative designs. Napkin rings have instant appeal because as well as being practical, they add originality and interest to a festive table. Use them as table decorations and then present them to your guests when the celebration ends.

The instructions show you how to make a pig napkin ring. The bird and elephant napkin rings use exactly the same cutout technique, but vary in shape and surface pattern. (You will find templates on page 140.)

When you decorate your napkin rings, either paint them to blend in with other table decorations, or make them stand out by using rich, contrasting colors.

Before beginning your project, please read "Materials and Techniques," pages 10–21.

TO MAKE THE PIG NAPKIN RING

MATERIALS AND EQUIPMENT
Salt dough (see page 12)
Dough paste (see page 13)
Nonstick baking sheet
Rolling pin
Ruler
Small kitchen knife
Small wooden spatula
Pig template (see page 140)
Paintbrushes for applying dough paste,
paints, and varnish
Rag or paper towel to apply paint finishes
Black and red water-based paints
Gloss polyurethane varnish

1 Roll dough to a thickness of ⅝ in. Place the pig template on top of the dough and, using the small kitchen knife, cut around the cardboard shape. Smooth any rough edges. Adjust any distortion in shape by patting gently with the flat edge of the knife or the spatula.

2 To make the pig's tail, roll a small piece of dough and bend it into a coil shape. Attach the tail to the pig using a little dough paste.

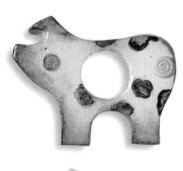

3 Bake the napkin ring, then turn the oven to a higher setting and brown the ring. Allow to cool.

4 Add spot details by dipping your finger into a small amount of black paint and dabbing it on. Do the same for the cheek (with a little red paint). When the paint has dried, varnish.

Homemade napkin rings and party favors make charming additions to any party table. The simple bird shape, above, was cut out from a template on page 140 and baked with the other animal rings featured on these pages. A rich base shade provides a contrasting background for a delicate gold pattern, applied with a fine-bristled brush, and layers of high-gloss varnish produce a lustrous sheen.

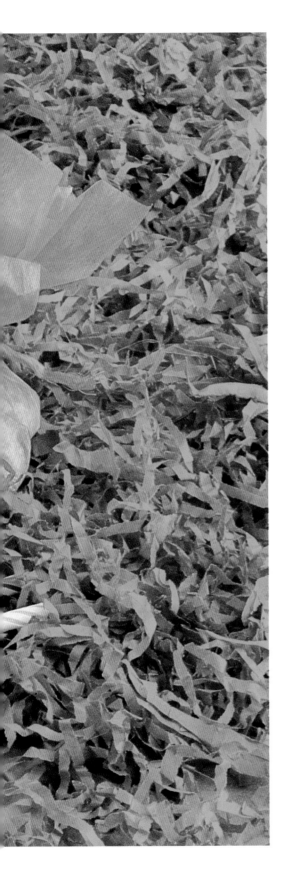

PIGLET HOUSE

A thatched cottage hiding three nursery-rhyme piglets is bound to appeal to anyone with a taste for surprises. This project makes a delightful table decoration for parties and celebrations, particularly if children are involved. Model extra piglets as party favors (one for each guest), or fill the house with candies and small gifts.

The house is simply molded over cardboard and decorated with fine strands of dough and surface scoring. Working with a three-dimensional shape is not difficult, but don't press too hard (particularly when scoring), in case you distort the dough. Transform the flat dough base into a colorful garden by applying a generous wash of green paint; then decorate the flower border in bright, cheerful shades.

Before beginning your project, please read "Materials and Techniques," pages 10–21. When varnishing your project, use a larger brush for the house and garden base and a smaller brush for the piglets. Small amounts of varnish, applied in thin, even layers produce the smoothest finish. Make sure that each coat is completely dry before applying the next.

MATERIALS AND EQUIPMENT

Salt dough (see page 12)
Dough paste (see page 13)
Nonstick baking sheet
Rolling pin
Ruler
Templates (page 141)
Small kitchen knife
Small wooden spatula
Aluminum foil
Cellophane or masking tape
Garlic press
Paintbrushes for applying dough paste,
paints, and varnish
Rag or paper towel to apply paint finishes
Water-based paints
Gloss polyurethane varnish

1 Using the cardboard template, make up the triangular mold for the piglet house. Secure tabs with tape. Carefully cover the cardboard completely with foil. Now smooth the foil to give a good, flat molding surface.

2 Roll out dough to a thickness of ¼ in. and carefully cover the mold. Trim off any excess dough. Smooth the surface and neaten rough edges.

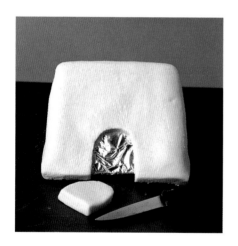

3 Cut a door shape out of the dough. Take care not to cut into the foil-covered mold underneath. Smooth rough edges and alter any overall distortion in shape.

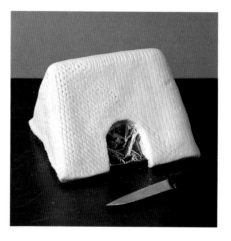

4 Using the knife, score all over the surface of the house. Working on one side of the house at a time, score straight, vertical lines followed by diagonal lines.

5 Squeeze balls of dough through the garlic press to make strands, about 2 in. long, for the roof. Use dough paste to attach the strands along the top of the house. Gently squeeze a clump of strands into a chimney shape and attach to the roof with dough paste. Arrange a few dough strands around the front door and attach them with dough paste.

6 Roll out more dough to a thickness of ¼ in. Lay the base template on top of the dough and cut around it. Smooth any rough surfaces. Push balls of dough through the garlic press. Laying down two or three strands at a time, make a narrow flower border around the base. Attach the strands to the base with dough paste.

7 Roll balls of dough by hand; attach them to the border with dough paste. Using the end of a paintbrush, indent the center of each ball. Now make petal shapes by scoring lines around the indentation. Model tiny leaves by flattening small balls of dough between your thumb and forefinger. Attach them to the border.

8 To make a piglet, roll two balls of dough, one slightly larger than the other. Stick them together with a little dough paste. Now attach a tiny ball for the nose, and indent it twice to make nostrils. Roll two small sausage shapes for ears and attach them with dough paste. The arms and legs are four small sausage shapes, attached with dough paste and scored for hooves. Roll a thin sausage and coil it into a tail. Attach the tail to the piglet with dough paste. Repeat to make more piglets.

9 Bake the base, the house, and the piglets. (Remember that smaller items will be ready sooner than larger pieces). When the pieces are cool, use the photograph as a guide for painting. When the paint is dry, varnish each part carefully.

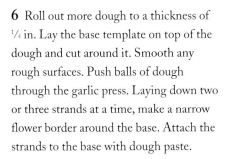

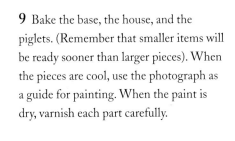

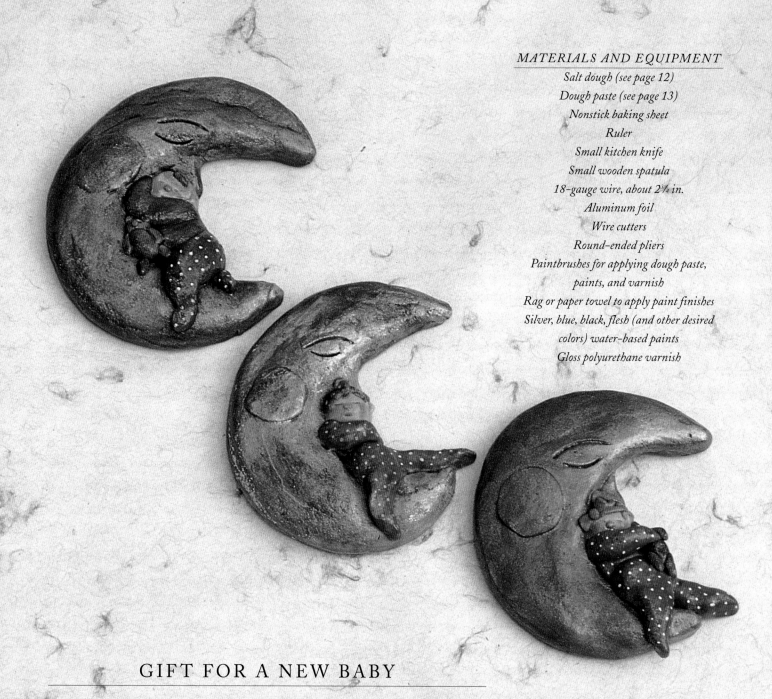

MATERIALS AND EQUIPMENT

Salt dough (see page 12)

Dough paste (see page 13)

Nonstick baking sheet

Ruler

Small kitchen knife

Small wooden spatula

18-gauge wire, about 2¼ in.

Aluminum foil

Wire cutters

Round-ended pliers

Paintbrushes for applying dough paste,
paints, and varnish

Rag or paper towel to apply paint finishes

Silver, blue, black, flesh (and other desired
colors) water-based paints

Gloss polyurethane varnish

GIFT FOR A NEW BABY

This sleeping infant cradled by a silver-blue moon makes a charming gift for a new baby.

Although modeling this project by hand is not difficult, it is best to take your time. Allow the step-by-step photographs and instructions to guide you, and try to keep the baby in proportion to the moon's size.

If you want to add something personal for the new baby, make a teddy bear or a toy for the salt dough baby to cuddle. Paint washes give the moon a shimmering glow, but when you paint the baby, use stronger colors as a contrast and apply details with a fine brush.

Before beginning, please read "Materials and Techniques," pp. 10–21.

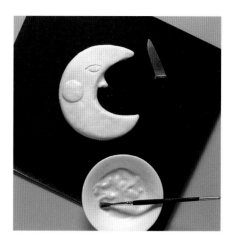

1 Working directly on the baking sheet, roll a very thick sausage of dough, about 12 in. long and about 2⅜ in. wide. Use the palm of your hand to squash and widen the dough and your fingers to tease the ends into points, making a moon shape.

2 Make a hanging loop from the wire. Turn the moon shape over and embed the ends of the loop into the moon, about ¾ in. above the center. Wedge a small, folded piece of foil behind the loop to prevent it from becoming embedded in the dough. Now turn the moon shape over again and adjust any change of shape.

3 Roll a cone of dough for the nose and squash it into shape. Attach it to the moon with dough paste, smoothing and blending it so that no joints are visible. (Attach all the features with dough paste.) Roll a small ball of dough and flatten it into a wide circle. Attach this cheek piece to the moon. Score in the moon's eye.

4 The baby's body is a sausage. Roll this by hand and gently press it into place in the lower horn of the moon. Roll a ball of dough for the baby's head. Attach it to the body by pressing gently; apply a little dough paste if necessary. (The baby's head should fit snugly under the moon's nose.)

5 Roll a sausage of dough for the arm and tease the end into a point. Position and attach. Make the legs by rolling two longer dough sausages. Tease the ends into points, position, and attach. The baby's ear and nose are tiny balls of dough. Attach them to the head shape. Score in the eyes and mouth. Make a bow from small sausages of dough. Position and attach.

6 Bake the plaque. When cool, paint the moon with washes of silver and blue. Dab on a little black paint and gently rub into the moon. Use brighter, contrasting colors for the baby's clothes and finish with tiny dots of white, applied with the point of a fine paintbrush. Use an almost-dry paintbrush to paint the baby's cheek. When the paint is dry, varnish your plaque.

MAKING TEMPLATES

The template shapes provided on pages 130–141 relate to many of the projects in the book. The instructions for these projects include page numbers for the appropriate templates.

Templates are extremely straightforward to make. Try not to rush the tracing and cutting processes, though —good, clean, neat-edged shapes give better results and can be used time and time again.

Photocopying is a quick alternative to tracing. Simply cut out photocopies of the template shapes, lay them on a piece of cardboard, and cut carefully around them.

MATERIALS

Cardboard – old cereal boxes are an ideal thickness, or buy sheets of card stock from stationers. Acetate is more expensive, but tends to last longer, and a wipe-clean surface is very useful when you are working with raw dough.
Sharp pencil
Craft knife, scalpel, or scissors
Tracing (or waxed) paper
Cutting mat

1 Using a soft pencil, trace shapes carefully onto tracing (or waxed) paper. Heavily shade over the outline.

2 Place the tracing on the cardboard face down and draw over the traced shape, pressing firmly enough to recreate the outline on the cardboard underneath.

3 Use a craft knife, scalpel, or scissors to cut out the cardboard shapes.

4 Roll out the dough to the desired thickness, place the template right side up on the dough, and cut around it carefully.

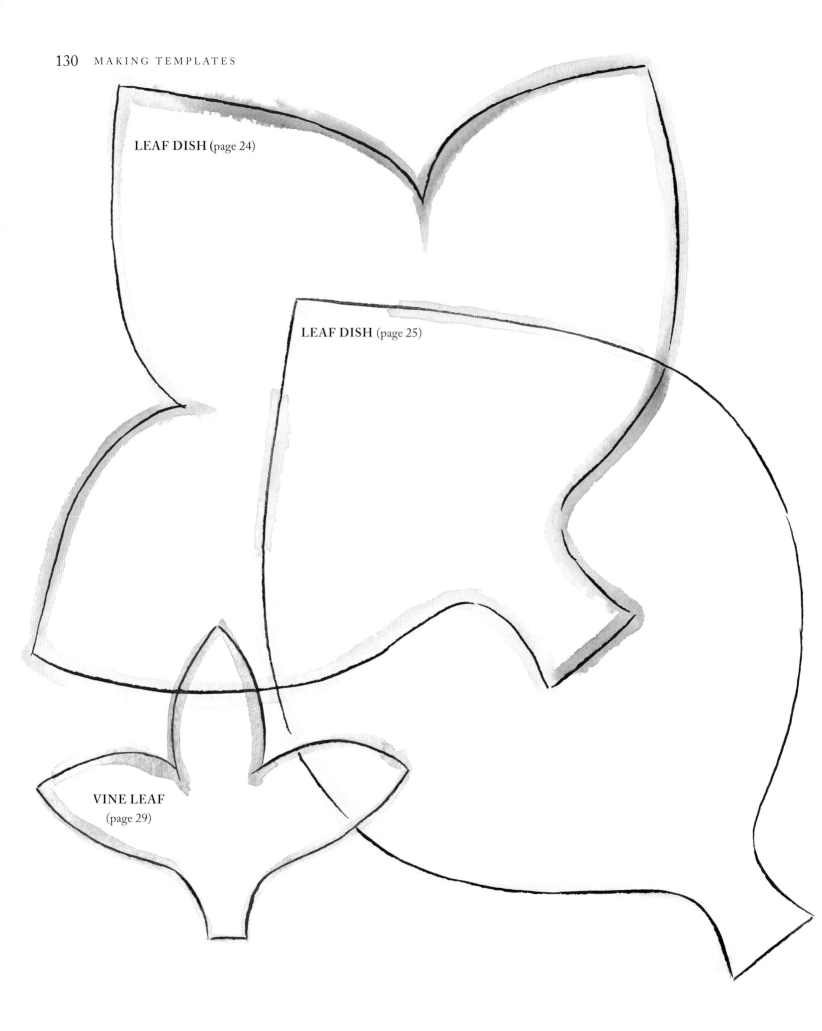

LEAF DISH (page 24)

LEAF DISH (page 25)

VINE LEAF
(page 29)

TRADITIONAL FRUIT BASKET (page 36)

BIRD (page 38)

HEART (page 38)

SMALL LEAF
(page 31)

SMALL LEAF
(page 36 and 92)

TOP

MOLDED SUN
(page 45)

MOLDED STAR
(page 43)

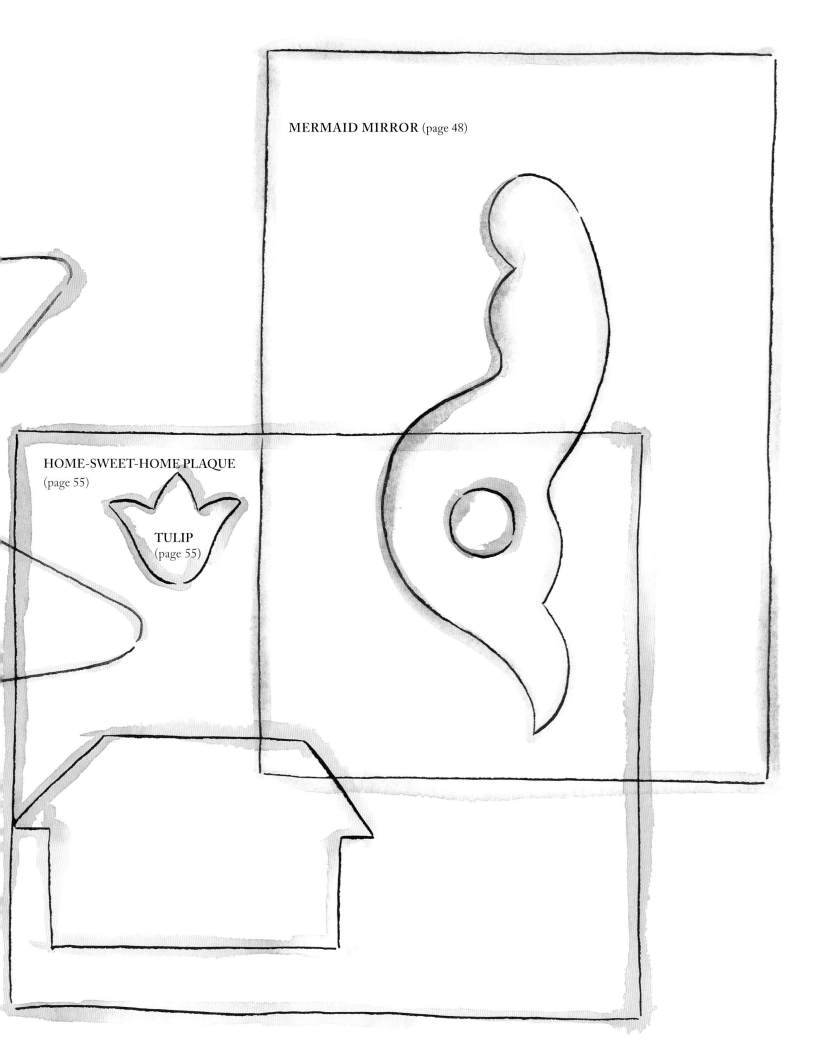

MERMAID MIRROR (page 48)

HOME-SWEET-HOME PLAQUE
(page 55)

TULIP
(page 55)

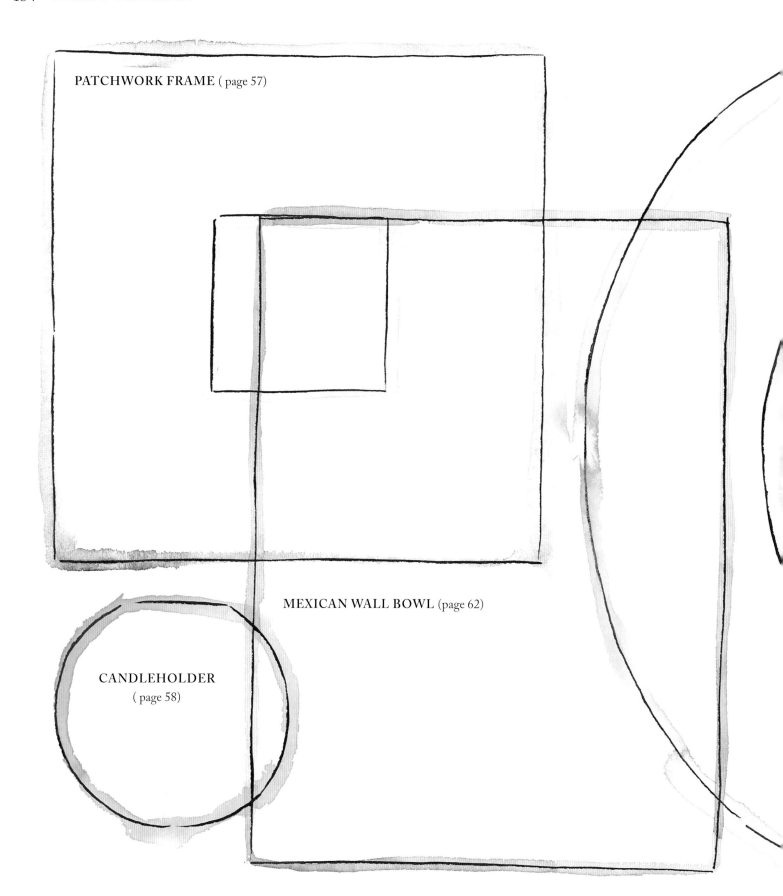

PATCHWORK FRAME (page 57)

MEXICAN WALL BOWL (page 62)

CANDLEHOLDER
(page 58)

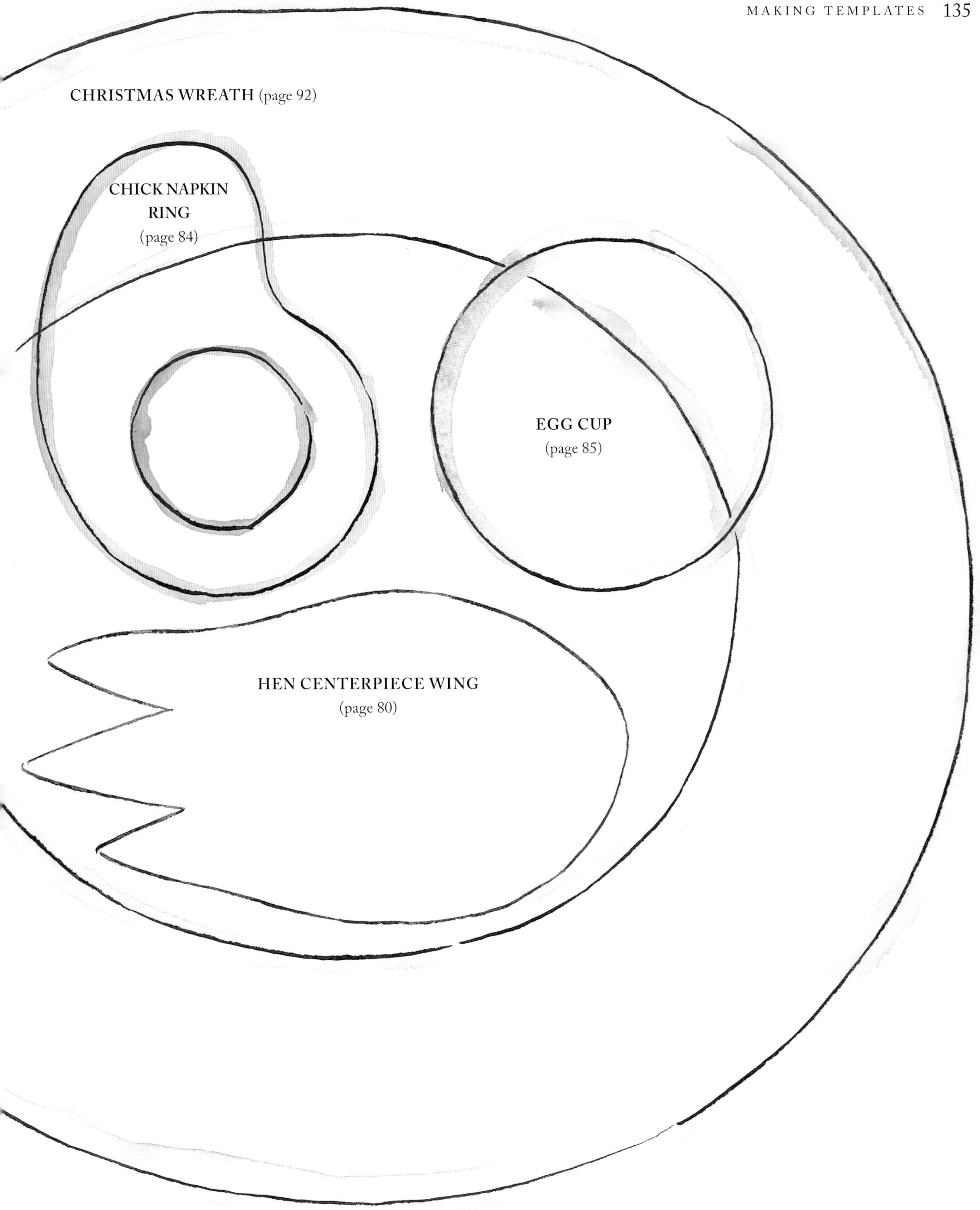

CHRISTMAS WREATH (page 92)

CHICK NAPKIN
RING
(page 84)

EGG CUP
(page 85)

HEN CENTERPIECE WING
(page 80)

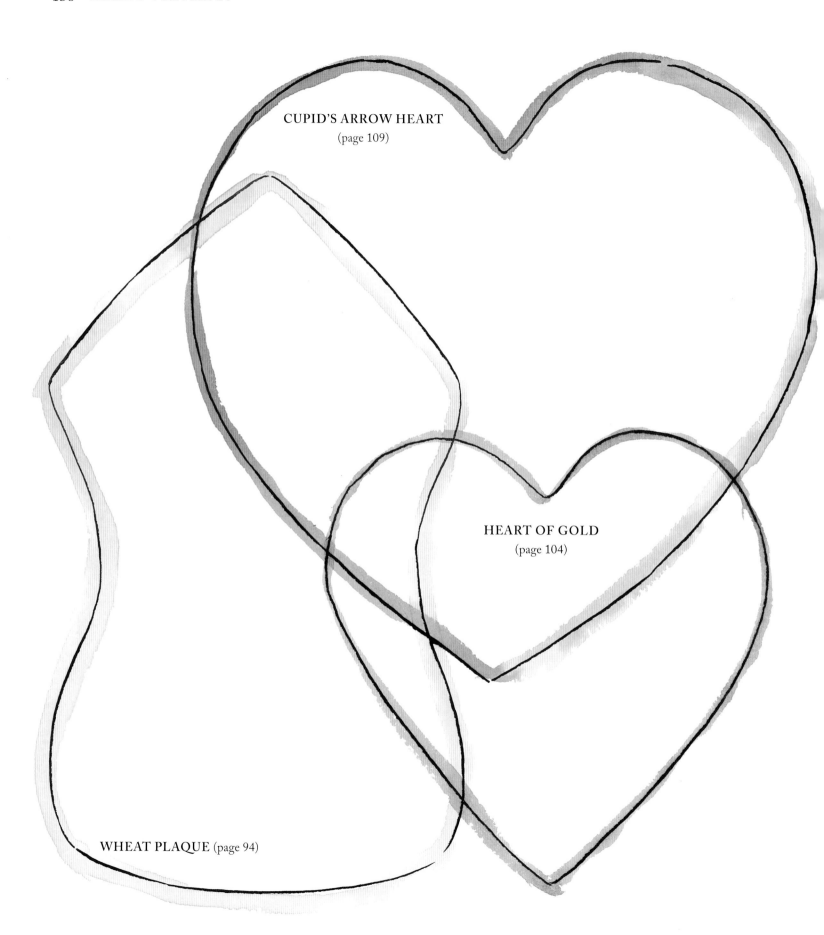

CUPID'S ARROW HEART
(page 109)

HEART OF GOLD
(page 104)

WHEAT PLAQUE (page 94)

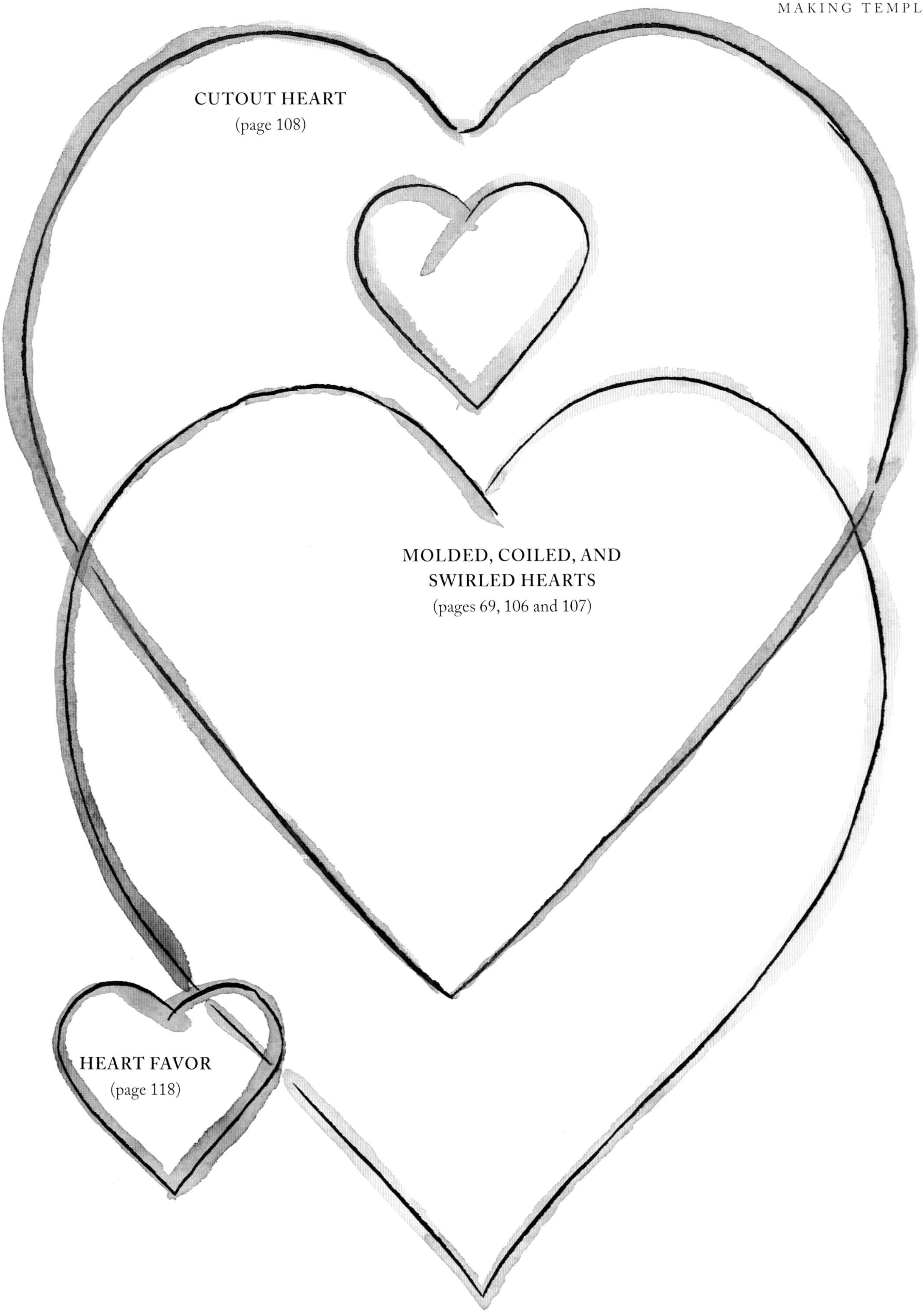

CUTOUT HEART
(page 108)

MOLDED, COILED, AND
SWIRLED HEARTS
(pages 69, 106 and 107)

HEART FAVOR
(page 118)

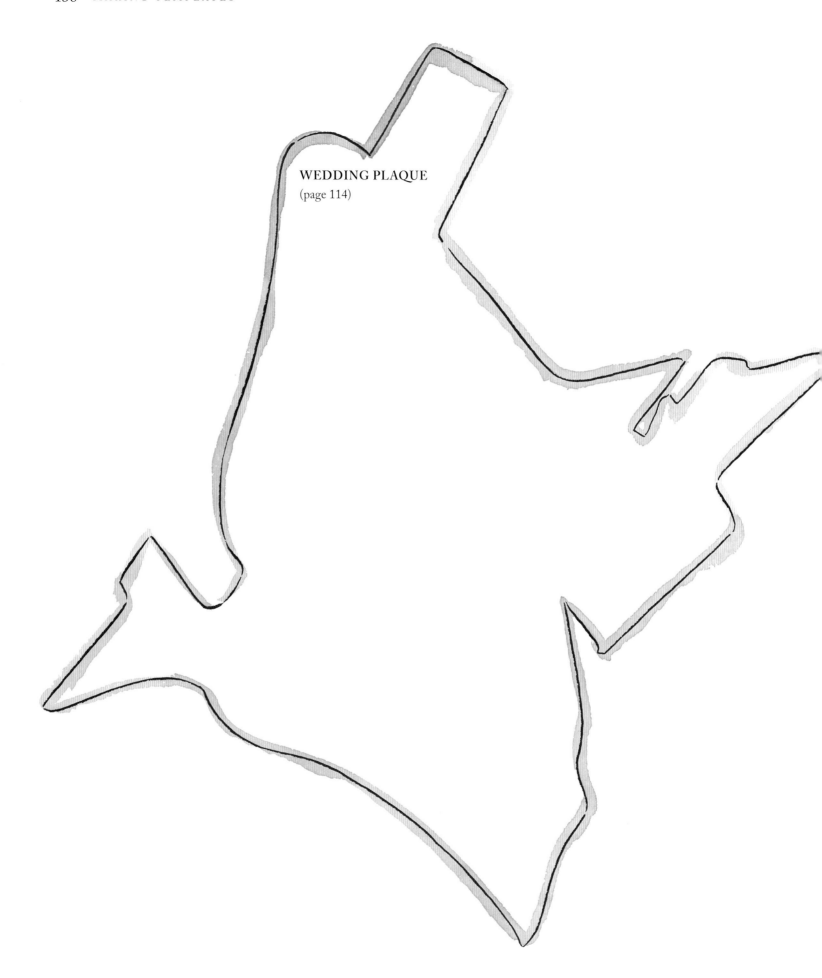

WEDDING PLAQUE
(page 114)

DOVE PLAQUE (page 113)

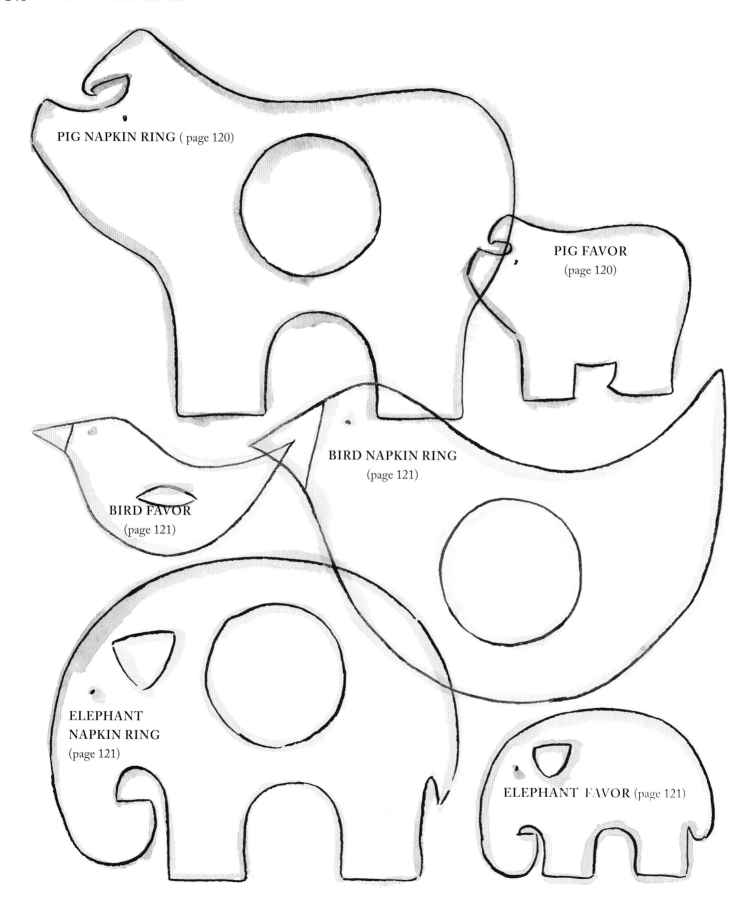

PIG NAPKIN RING (page 120)

PIG FAVOR
(page 120)

BIRD NAPKIN RING
(page 121)

BIRD FAVOR
(page 121)

ELEPHANT
NAPKIN RING
(page 121)

ELEPHANT FAVOR (page 121)

**PIGLET HOUSE
BASE**
see page 124

FOLD

FOLD

PIGLET HOUSE (page 124)

FOLD

FOLD

FOLD

FOLD

INDEX

ACKNOWLEDGMENTS

The publishers and authors would like to thank the following people
for their help and support in the production of this book:

Michael Hill for the template illustrations

Blake Minton for her help with the styling

Janine Tilley for her hospitality during the step-by-step photoshoot